Taken

STOLEN LIVES

Taken

A true story of the pain and
scandal of forced adoption

MICHELLE PEARSON
with EVE HATTON

MARDLE

First published in 2022 by Mardle Books
15 Church Road
London, SW13 9HE
www.mardlebooks.com

Text © 2022 Michelle Pearson

Paperback ISBN 9781914451768

eBook ISBN 9781914451775

A CIP catalogue record for this book is available from the British Library.

Every reasonable effort has been made to trace copyright-holders of
material reproduced in this book, but if any have been inadvertently
overlooked the publishers would be glad to hear from them.

Design and typesetting by Danny Lyle

Printed in the UK

10 9 8 7 6 5 4 3 2 1

Cover image: Getty

Foreword

Michelle's story is a deeply private tragedy. It is a story of loss and enduring pain after her son was taken from her and placed for adoption in 1972 because she was unmarried. Social and parental pressure combined with the expertise of the authorities steered Michelle towards adoption as the best course of action for her and her son. Aged just sixteen, she complied. This book is more than a story of just that moment. The anguish of her decision and the impact it has on her life leap off every page. Equally compelling is Michelle's reunion with her son and rebuilding of her life with him and his family.

Michelle's story is also part of a public scandal; the story of tens of thousands of mothers having children outside of marriage. The same pressures and judgements were applied, pushing for the adoption of their children by 'normal' families being in the best interests of everyone. Choice was illusory. Any hope of Michelle keeping her son would have been surrounded with shame and stigma. The anguish Michelle felt was never felt by the authorities; the lifelong impact dismissed. Her story provides unique and compelling reasons why this needs to change.

Dr Michael Lambert

Valentine's Day, 1972

Standing at the door of the day nursery I hold my breath, as if by doing so I can freeze this moment in time forever. I'm not supposed to be here. I'm supposed to be upstairs in the dormitory I share with three other girls, packing my few personal belongings into a bag. I'm going home this afternoon. Home. Back to normal life. Though how can life ever be normal again after today?

Glancing around to make sure no-one's watching, I slip through the nursery door and there he is – my son, my Baby Tim – in his crib just inside to the left. I gaze at him in absolute adoration as he sleeps on fresh white linen. He's dressed in a white layette to match, pristine and new. His sleeping face is serene and beautiful. His peach-soft cheeks were made to be stroked. He looks like an angel from a story book and every time I see him, my heart seems to grow a little bigger. I didn't know my very being could be so connected and intertwined with another's or that I could love someone this much.

Though it's cold outside, the pale winter sun streams in through the nursery windows and warms my face as if to comfort me. Much as I long to, I can't pick my baby up and cradle him in my arms. I didn't put him in those bright white clothes. They're not for my benefit either. My baby has been dressed for his own journey away from this place and away from me. At any moment, a social worker will arrive to take him to a foster family. I don't know where he'll be going after that.

It's as if a sheet of glass has already descended between us and all I can do is press my hands against it and whisper, 'Goodbye, my darling son, my baby Tim. I love you. I love you so much. I want to stay. I want to hold you close and never let you go…'

I want to call out in pain – this moment taking me back to a memory of another girl leaving while I was still pregnant, her cries of anguish echoing up through the house as she was physically dragged away from her child. In my moment of goodbye, I share the same agony. I will turn and walk away with my own cries of anguish, the only difference being that mine are held deep within me where no-one but me can hear them.

With one last look at my Baby Tim's sleeping face, I force myself to step away. The words of Sister Dolores echo in my mind, 'Go away from here and get on with your life, Michelle. Just forget that you had a baby. Remember you are doing the best thing for your child.'

She's right. I'm a bad girl. I'm one of 'those girls'. I'm not a real mother, so I'm doing the only thing I can. I'm doing the 'best thing'. I'm giving up my baby so that he can have a better life without me.

'I'm sorry,' I whisper one last time. I hold my pain deep in my soul and do my best not to scream in despair as I leave.

Stepping out into the corridor on that cold February morning, holding back tears no-one will wipe away, I'm sure I'll never see my son again.

Chapter One

This is a story of love and loss: the loss of my baby, the loss of my innocence, the loss of the life I might have had – stolen from me, taken and buried in a culture of corrosive secrecy that led to decades of shame and self-doubt. It's a story that's still unfolding as, 50 years on from the day I gave my son up for adoption, new fragments of the past continue to come to the surface. Even in the course of writing this book, I've uncovered long hidden facts that might have changed everything had I known them in 1972. But that year, I was just a 16-year-old schoolgirl, facing the might of centuries-old social and religious institutions with very clear ideas as to how someone like me should behave. An unmarried mother should not keep her child.

But it wasn't only the chance to be a mother that was taken from me the day I said 'goodbye' to my Baby Tim. To give you a sense of how much I actually lost when I gave up my son, it's perhaps best to start with where I came from...

I was born in the summer of 1955, as the United Kingdom bathed in a glorious heatwave. My arrival, a month earlier than expected, was greeted with much jubilation. My father was a

Flying Officer in the RAF and his air crew were determined that my birth be properly celebrated. Dad's crew were like brothers to him. They all knew how much he'd longed for a family of his own, so on the day of my birth, they took him out on the town, toasting my mother and me in every pub on the high street. They sang and cheered as they walked along arm in arm. There was no doubt that everyone involved agreed my birth was something to sing about.

'You're a dad, blessed with a baby girl!'

I imagine Dad at the end of the raucous evening, stumbling back to his married quarters on the RAF station with a huge smile on his face, already making future plans for his much-wanted baby daughter. What would I grow up to be? Would I be an artist or a scientist? An academic or someone with practical skills? Whichever path I chose, he was sure I would make him proud.

Every new parent has great hopes for their first child but perhaps my parents had greater expectations than most. From the outside, Mum and Dad were the quintessentially English-sounding Mr and Mrs Pearson, however their family name hid a complicated history. It might have been wonderful to be welcoming a new baby in the English summertime, but their lives so far had taught them that things weren't always so easy, so uncomplicated, or so happy.

Dad was Polish, He was conceived and born during the 1918-1919 Polish Ukrainian war. His family lived in abject poverty and he was an unwanted child. As he grew up malnourishment affected his development and stunted his growth. He would talk of only having shoes in the winter months and of his five-mile daily walk to school.

In 1939 when the Soviets and the Nazis carved Poland up between them, Dad joined the Polish Army. He told me that in the spring of 1940, he had witnessed the notorious Katyn Massacre, in which more than 20,000 Polish officers and members of the intelligentsia were killed upon Stalin's orders. Soon after that, Dad was captured by the Russians and sent to a prisoner of war camp in Siberia. Conditions were brutal. They left him starving and weak. Then in 1941 Germany invaded the USSR; the Soviets joined the Allies and with the support of Anthony Eden, the British Foreign Secretary, the Sikorski-Mayski military agreement came into effect. In August that year, amnesty was granted to Polish citizens and POWs were enlisted to allied forces.

Dad was enlisted in December 1941, ready for evacuation to Iraq. I cannot imagine what it must have been like for him. I know that in the labour camp he had developed night blindness, nicknamed 'chicken eyes', as a result of chronic malnourishment. This meant that every day once the sun went down he was blind until the following sunrise. How did he manage to survive making the journey to the Middle East, already so weakened? Many thousands died.

In May 1942 Dad arrived in Iraq. In September that year, he was one of a group of 220 recruits transferred from the Polish Army to the Polish Airforce, destined to join the RAF in England. *The Devonshire* took him by sea to Karachi, with onward travel several months later, first to Bombay, India and then to Durban in South Africa. As he set sail from South Africa, little did he know his life was to be threatened again. On March 13th 1943, his ship, *The Empress of Canada*, was torpedoed and sunk by an Italian submarine.

Dad spent almost four days in the water before being rescued by a Royal Navy Destroyer. Approximately 400 people died. Dad told me he was lucky; when the ship got hit, he was covered in engine oil and this formed a protective barrier between him and the cold salt water of the Atlantic. Nevertheless, when he was picked up he was unable to stand up as his bones were so weak. After a short period of recuperation in Freetown, he finally arrived in Liverpool, disembarking from the *Mauretania* at the end of March 1943.

This was the start of a new chapter in Dad's life filled with danger and courage. After completing his radio operator training, in July 1944 he was assigned to 18 OTU for his flying training with pilot Flying Officer Kozuba-Kozubski. I mention him by name as after qualifying this crew moved to 300 Squadron, part of Bomber Command. Between 27th November 1944 to 25th April 1945 they completed and survived 30 missions together. The life expectancy of the air crews of Bomber Command was often brutally short. They looked death square in the face every time they took to the air.

Dad told me he once returned from a mission to discover that he was the only man from his Nissen hut to have survived the night. I often wonder if this was 2nd March 1945 when records show the heavy loss of 14 members of his squadron. That hut full of empty beds must have been a heart-breaking sight.

Post war Dad was commissioned in the RAF where he stayed until retirement at 55 years of age. His flying career, in a multitude of plane types including: Wellington, Lancaster, Halifax, Dakota, York, Britannia, Valetta, Varsity and Hastings, took him all over the globe including into several post WWII conflict zones and to the nuclear tests at Christmas Island, known as Operation Grapple. For a while he was also assigned to RAF Northolt as part of VIP qualified aircrew. After completing close to 5000 flying hours he moved to Air Traffic Control until his retirement at which point he retrained to become a plumber.

* * *

My mother's journey to life as Mrs Pearson on an English RAF station also began in Eastern Europe. She was born in Estonia. Her family were comfortably off, owning a shop, a mill and possibly dress-making or tailor-related businesses. But like Dad, Mum saw her plans for her future ripped up by the war. In 1940 Estonia was occupied by the Russians and later in 1941 by the Germans, before reoccupation by the Soviets in 1944.

During the German occupation around 6000 ethnic Estonians were killed in addition to around 1000 with Jewish heritage. Mum survived but was taken to Germany. I know very little about this, where she went or what happened to her. She only talked about working in a German household, and later living on her wits with two other young Estonian women. All three were passing as Germans and carrying false papers. No mean feat given that one of them could not speak German at all. They had to pretend she was deaf and mute.

On the 13th and 14th of February 1945 Mum was in Dresden as it was bombed by UK and American forces. Estimates of civilian casualties vary enormously with some sources citing 25,000 - 30,000. By all accounts it was apocalyptic in nature with the bombs creating a firestorm. I have no idea how Mum made it out alive or indeed how she travelled away. Thankfully by the end of the war she had moved north-west and was in the British occupation zone.

I can only surmise that Mum came to the UK on the 'European Volunteer Worker' (EVW) scheme between 1946-47, which specifically asked for women as domestic workers in hospitals and other institutions. I have a vague memory of Mum describing her first job in the UK as a hospital cleaner. The scheme paid 24/6d as a settling in allowance, issued a ration card and clothing coupons. Board and lodgings were provided in hostel type accommodation. EVWs were denied formal refugee status, yet classed as 'suitable immigrants'. They were constantly under threat of deportation as their work permits were subject to annual renewals based on satisfactory service. What a fragile and vulnerable position my mother and other EVWs were in. Formally classed as aliens under the 1905 Act they also had to report to the Police if they changed occupation or address. And there was hostility towards them from the local population as EVWs were seen as a threat to jobs and levels of pay.

It's hard to fill in many more details. Neither of my parents spoke much about their wartime experiences or dwelled on the hardships they'd experienced. Mum in particular was very firm about it, telling me if I asked, 'Yesterday is in the past. You can't change anything about it so why talk about it now?' It was an attitude she maintained her entire life. I did however manage to glean that Mum met Dad while she was working as a housekeeper at a hotel in Eastbourne. Dad was there on leave from a 'Government Service' role he had been recruited for some time after the end of WWII. He was involved in various cold war operations; roles which were only ever undertaken by single men. It is no wonder that they were ready to let off steam during their 'R&R'. He and his friends were trying in vain to ride a tricycle while under the influence of a few too many beers! Mum was not impressed, but somehow it brought them together.

After all the fears my parents had faced during the war and the frustration of their youthful hopes and dreams, it's perhaps no surprise that they desperately wanted to settle down and to build a 'normal' life in England. However, this presented a challenge for them. My father's Government

Service role precluded him from getting married. He had already had to anglicise his surname and agree to cut off all contact with his surviving family members back in Poland. Having an Eastern European wife would have put him at risk and the service was adamant – they were not to be married. Thankfully, my father persevered and after much difficulty agreement was reached and my parents had their wedding. It was at this point that my father was transferred to the regular RAF and commissioned with the rank of Flying Officer.

While extremely proud of their heritage, they wanted to be as British as they could be; to become established members of the society they respected, and to embrace its culture. Both my parents were starting their life together in Britain in vulnerable positions in the face of potential hostility and unfavourable attitudes. Post war attitudes had shifted away from Poles being brave and courageous allies. My mother was already used to hostility. They were soulmates and wanted to do things properly. They wanted me to grow up as a solid UK citizen.

Dad also wanted me to grow up as a good Catholic. Despite the many moments in his youth when it must have seemed as though God had forgotten all about him, he was a staunch Catholic. Having been raised in the strict Lutheran church, Mum had abandoned Christianity during the war and become an atheist. As I understand it, in order for Mum to be able to marry a practicing Catholic, my parents had to seek agreement from the Bishop, and Mum had to agree to any children being christened and raised as Catholics. The fact that I was given not one, or even two, but *four* Christian names (in honour of my grandmothers and earlier female lineage) underlines how much I was expected to carry the family history and create a future of which my parents and their forebears could be proud; a weight which would prove very heavy on my young shoulders.

Chapter Two

Unlike many fathers in the 1950s, Dad was very involved with looking after me when he was at home, giving me bottles and changing my nappies without complaint. The challenge was that being air crew, he wasn't very often at home. Though he had some time off to be with Mum and me immediately after my birth, he was soon away on detachment again.

Dad might be sent anywhere, UK or overseas, and a detachment could last for several months. He must have spent quite a bit of my first few years away, because my mother often told this story from when I was around three years old: apparently, she and I were walking down Chichester High Street together when I suddenly started calling out to every man we passed, 'Daddy? Daddy? Daddy?'

Having not seen my father for a while, I couldn't remember clearly what he looked like, so I'd decided I would just keep asking until I found him. My mother was very embarrassed. What if people thought I didn't have a father in my life? Mum was a respectable married woman. The last thing she wanted was for people to think she didn't have a husband to go with her child.

As a young girl, I was what you might have called a 'handful' and I kept my mother on her toes. On one occasion, when she and I were in the garden together, I ran back into the house and locked the door from the inside so that she couldn't get back in. No matter how she coaxed and threatened through the letterbox, I would not open that door. Mum obviously understood the danger of my being alone in a house full of hazards like the stove, the fire and the stairs but it was all just a great game to me.

On another occasion, as we were moving house to a place I didn't think much of, I ran away from home. While the removal men and my parents were unloading the van I gathered a few of my favourite toys under my arm and was off down the road before Mum could catch me. I would often hide from my parents, enjoying their exasperation as they hunted high and low to find me. I didn't sleep much and when I was awake I was always full of energy. I was bold and cheeky and I enjoyed being the centre of attention; the apple of my father's eye.

Four and a half years after I was born, my sister Christine came along. I was very happy to be an only child and did not greet Christine's arrival with enthusiasm. When Mum showed me my new baby sister for the first time, my first words on the subject were characteristically blunt, 'Take her outside, put her in the dustbin, put the lid on and put a stone on the top.' I obviously felt usurped – I was no longer the centre of my parents' universe. I did not want to share.

It was not long after Christine was born that I started school. I loved school from the very first day, quickly settling in and making friends, but just three weeks into my first term, we were on the move again. Dad was to be posted to Singapore and we were going to join him. Poor Mum had to pack up the whole house on her own, while looking after two small children. I didn't make life any easier for my parents. Having taken one look at the needles laid out in readiness to give me the jabs we needed to be able to travel overseas, I bolted from the GP's surgery and had to be chased up the road by the doctor and Dad!

When we arrived in Singapore, the house in Changi where we were to live was not yet ready, so we were temporarily housed at the legendary Raffles hotel. The glamorous colonial-era hotel, which looked like a gigantic white wedding cake, was a paradise compared to our house back on the RAF station in England and I loved the month we had there, spending my days happily jumping in and out of the beautiful swimming pool.

Unfortunately, my extended holiday had to come to an end with the start of term at the RAF school at Changi. Though I'd enjoyed my first experience of school back in England, I was so outraged by the idea that I had to go to school again, when I could be playing in the pool, that I refused to go. I had to be carried there by one of my father's RAF colleagues – including through the hotel – kicking and screaming all the way. Once in the classroom, however, I soon settled down again, enjoying the routine of mornings in lessons and afternoons off (happily back by the pool). My first report from the RAF Children's Primary School in Singapore declared me, 'Pleasant, co-operative and conscientious.' That must have been a big relief for my parents…

In Singapore, Dad continued to practice his Catholic faith but for the first time, I learned that Dad's religion was not the only one. Having heard a group of children singing beautifully, I wanted to join their choir. However, this particular choir was affiliated to the Church of England. When the choirmaster asked me about my faith, I assured him that I was definitely C of E and he believed me. My parents agreed to me joining, as nothing had been said about the choir's religious affiliations and I kept quiet. All went well until after a performance when my parents were waiting to collect me. With the vicar standing outside among the choir members, I quickly hid behind another singer. I'm not sure how I thought I would get away with this, as at some point I had to go to the car and my secret was out. Mum might have found it amusing that I was pretending to be a Protestant – she was still very much an atheist – but I'm sure Dad did not.

Singapore was also a time and place for me as a five-year-old to learn a harsh reality of life. Every week a children's film would be screened by the side of the RAF pool and before the film we would play bingo. I got off to a good start and for several weeks in a row, I came home with a prize. Then one week my numbers didn't come up, and I came home empty handed. I sobbed my little heart out not really understanding how this could be so. I genuinely believed that every week meant a prize for me.

One day, I think it was in 1961 when I was coming up to six, my father went to work expecting to join a crew flying on an exercise, as he had done many times before. Mum thought nothing much of it – I'm sure she was busy with my sister and me – until a 'breaking news' bulletin on Forces Radio announced that the plane our father was scheduled to join had gone down, with every crew member lost. How shocked and scared Mum must have been as she gathered my sister and me together to tell us the bad news. How alone she must have felt as she gently told us we would never see our Daddy again.

But the news had barely begun to sink in when our father walked through the door, still very much alive. For some reason, Dad's commanding officer had taken him off the crew that boarded the fatal flight that morning. It was a last-minute decision that saved his life.

The air crash incident was not the only time in my childhood that it seemed we were going to be a one-parent family. During that same period, our mother had to be flown back to the UK as an emergency, for treatment for an illness that was probably cancer. My sister and I were not told the details of her condition, but I distinctly remember being told that she was going to die. It seemed there was no sugar-coating these things in the 1960s. It might have been a generational thing. Thanks to the war, Mum and Dad's peers were used to taking loss on the chin and my parents had perfected the art of the stiff upper lip.

Perhaps it was because of our mother's illness that I was sent to boarding school at the age of nine. Due to the nature of RAF life, I had already attended three or four different primary schools by then, getting used to making friends quickly then moving on and starting again with a new set. However, my parents had never before considered actually sending me away to school.

Nine years old might be considered early to begin boarding now, but according to my family, it was what I wanted and I was keen to go. Mum and Dad felt that it would be good for me to have some continuity of education too. The RAF must have paid my fees, in order that Dad could keep working while Mum was not well enough to care for Christine and me. I know my parents could not have afforded for me to be a boarder otherwise.

The Convent of the Sacred Heart of Mary in Hillingdon was extremely posh. I boarded weekly, going home for the weekends. Every Friday afternoon the car park was full of smart new cars, as parents arrived to pick their daughters up. There were big Bentleys and Rollers, shining as though they'd been driven straight from the showroom forecourt. My father's old Volkswagen Beetle must have looked very out of place.

I have only good memories of my time at the Convent of the Sacred Heart. I was eager to learn and my termly reports echoed those from Singapore. I was a polite, helpful and happy child. One teacher even called me 'lady-like', which if you knew me is extraordinary! We had lessons in deportment and elocution to polish up our social skills. I was great at maths. I was 'a pleasure to teach' and 'enthusiastic and eager to learn.' The only possible problems were that I was occasionally 'disorderly' in my work and, in 1966, was bottom of the class for the state of my handwriting. But I was a model pupil and a model daughter, living up to the expectations of my teachers and my parents, who could not have been more pleased.

This was also a time when I found myself in hospital. I had been born with a squint that, for whatever reason, was not dealt with until I was 10 (I don't remember it affecting me in any way, at least not in terms of being teased or ridiculed by others at school). I was used to being away from home, but this was different. I had no idea what was going to happen to me.

From my mum's illness, I knew that hospitals were places you went to when you might die. These days I expect children are prepared for what's going be done to them. Back then I'm not so sure. Years later my parents would share a story of my hospital experience with amusement. Apparently, it had taken six male medics in the hospital at RAF Halton to hold me down and keep me still enough for whatever was being done to me. I must have been terrified!

Back at school, my father's academic expectations for me were always high. During conversations we've had as adults, my sister Christine has said that, growing up four years behind me, she did not feel the same pressure to succeed academically. Mum and Dad's ambitions for her were more orientated towards her raising a family. It's ironic then that I saw Christine as a goody-two shoes, who liked nothing more than to sit quietly reading or doing her art work, while outside school I was always in trouble for exploring. I loved to be outdoors. I was always pushing boundaries. Christine would just smile when I got into trouble.

In the seventies, a television series called *The Good Life* would sum up the difference between me and my sister. I was Barbara, always up to my knees in mud and with straw in my hair. Christine was the tidy, refined and elegant Margot who looked at Barbara with incredulity.

It was while I was at school in Hillingdon that another sister, Anna, came along. Little Anna was born three months premature, weighing just 2lbs and 1oz when she came into the world. She was impossibly tiny and it seemed there was little hope she would survive. My parents were distraught in the early weeks after her birth. Care for premature babies was not as sophisticated as it is now and most didn't make it. But Anna did make it. She came home and we were a family of five.

Chapter Three

In the summer of 1966, I passed the 'eleven plus' exam, meaning I could have a place at the local state grammar school. However, Dad's job meant we were on the move again. We had to leave Hillingdon and head west to an RAF station about seven miles from Bath – RAF Colerne – where Dad would be working in Air Traffic Control, having retired from flying.

These days, we think of Bath as a particularly beautiful city, with all those elegant Regency buildings in creamy Bath stone shining in the sunlight. In the 1960s, it wasn't quite like that. When Dad drove us around, I saw for the first time a block of flats. Not quite high-rise, but taller than anything I had seen. The Bath stone of the regency buildings was black with soot and there were areas that were very rundown. I remember being unimpressed, but if there was one thing I knew how to do, thanks to our RAF lifestyle, it was turn up somewhere new and settle in without a fuss.

RAF Colerne, where we would be living, was a relatively large station. It had a NAAFI store, as well stocked as any city centre supermarket, and a sports centre with a swimming pool. It even had its own cinema. The station's housing was divided into four estates, on which accommodation was allocated according to rank.

We lived in married quarters on the estate for junior officers. We were given a semi-detached house with three bedrooms. I had a room of my own and plastered the walls with posters from *Jackie* magazine, which was the big teen magazine at the time. I remember having a particularly big poster of *The Monkees*, an American band, formed as the basis for a children's TV show, who soon became popular as musicians in their own right. I also liked Mungo Jerry and the solo artist Donovan. I knew all the words to his songs, I especially liked *Catch the Wind* and *Universal Soldier*.

There were many children on the station and there was always someone to hang out with. The station was a great place for children. There was a dedicated playground between the middle two estates, which attracted youngsters from all over. We also made the assault course where the RAF Regiment trained on weekdays our adventure playground at the weekends. There was no such thing as 'health and safety' and we climbed and swung from ropes to our heart's delight, never worrying about the dangers.

On Saturday mornings, we would go to the cinema for a special children's showing. At home, we had a black and white television, on which Christine and I would watch *The Man From UNCLE* and *Doctor Who*. I was a great fan of *Doctor Who*, which appealed to my love of things scientific.

With my love of swimming from our time in Singapore, I'd spend as much time as I could in the pool. I also made extra pocket money by looking after people's pets. I remember in particular dog-sitting for a family that had a Pyrenean Mountain Dog, a huge beast, that seemed as big as a small horse to me. Though their dog was enormous, their family car was a Mini, and with two children on board there was no room to take their pet on days out too. The dog stayed with me on the station.

Having spent the summer settling in, I looked forward to the beginning of a new school term. Instead of the local grammar school, I was going to attend La Sainte Union Convent School, known more casually as Bath Convent. I was eager to get there and start making another set of new friends. Life felt like a great big adventure.

Chapter Four

Bath Convent was a girls' catholic school. The school was private, but it was what was known as 'direct grant', which meant that the local authority paid the fees of catholic girls who had passed their 11+ and would be attending for religious reasons (such as I would). It was set in the grounds of the imposing Convent of La Sainte Union on the city's Pulteney Road.

I remember my first sight of the building where I would be a pupil for the next five years – seven if I passed my O-levels. It was far bigger than any school I had attended before; a serious place of learning. Here I would get the sort of education my parents had been denied by world events. Having been a big fish in the small pond that was The Sacred Heart of Mary in Hillingdon, I felt a little awed as I imagined joining the pupils here. The Bath Convent girls seemed so grown-up and sophisticated.

On my first day, I proudly wore my uniform, which included a smart maroon blazer. During winter terms, we wore that blazer with a matching skirt, shirt and tie. During the summer, we wore it over a breezy yellow cotton poplin dress. We convent girls were always impeccably accessorised. Felt hat in winter, straw boater in the summer. Gloves when we were out in public; maroon in winter and pure white in summer.

The nuns would measure the length of our skirts to make sure that we were 'decent'. Skirts were not to be shorter than one inch above the knee. If a nun with a ruler found that your skirt was not regulation length, she would use that same ruler to smack you hard across the palms. If you'd just rolled your skirt up at the waistband (as we all did at times, to look more fashionable), you'd have to roll it back down. If you'd gone so far as to sew your hem up, the hem would be ripped so that the skirt fell to the right length again. We were strictly forbidden from eating while in uniform outside school. Standards were high both inside and outside the gates.

For lessons, we were split into three streams, named X, Y and W. The stream named X was the 'top' stream. The pupils in X were considered the most academically gifted and their lesson options were chosen accordingly. I was in the Y Stream, the middle stream, which meant that my syllabus was a mixture of the academic and the vocational. I had to study Latin and Needlework but my real passion was science. As an eight-year-old, I'd proudly told anyone who cared to ask that I wanted to be a 'lavatory assistant' when I grew up. I meant 'laboratory' of course. Now on the verge of my teens, I was fascinated by astronomy, often gazing up at the night sky in the hope of discovering a new star.

Just as at my boarding school in Hillingdon, I fitted in at the Convent from the start and my early reports reveal that I was doing well academically, even if my written work wasn't always as organised as my teachers would have liked.

I was a good all-rounder. I was keen on sport – especially netball and hockey – and played on the school teams. I was always on 'attack', playing goal shoot in netball and right inner at hockey. My cohort at the Convent was fortunate that our sports teacher was an early proponent of women's cricket, so we got to play that too. Outside school, I trained as a lifeguard at the RAF station's swimming pool and I became a patrol leader for the guides. I was very community-minded, someone who liked to 'join in'.

Though I'd been a cheeky child, as I grew up and became a teenager, I always did my best to fit in and comply with the expectations of the adults around me. In the 1960s, parenting was very different to the way it is now. Children weren't given room to think and choose for themselves as they are today. Your parents told you what you believed and you didn't question it. Simple as that. The freedom of the 'swinging sixties' did not apply to me.

As a young girl at Bath Convent, I definitely believed in my parents' values. On Sundays Christine and I went to church with Dad. Mum had stuck by her promise that she would support him raising us in his religion. I even remember having to go to Saturday morning Catechism classes when I was not being taught in a catholic school. I'd been through my christening and then my 'first communion' while in Singapore. At the convent, I completed my initiation into the Catholic faith upon receipt of the third sacrament, that of Confirmation. I was well and truly a Catholic now.

There's a photograph of me with Dad from around this time. We're both of us in uniform – his RAF, mine school – and we're being presented to a Catholic bishop. I am gazing up at the tall man in his ecclesiastical robes with a look of absolute awe.

Incidentally, Bath Convent is the alma mater of a very well-known Catholic: Anne Widdecombe, the former conservative MP and cabinet minister, famous for entertaining the nation with her clumsy quickstep on *Strictly Come Dancing* but also for her old-fashioned views on abortion, LGBTQ+ rights and the death penalty. As an MP Miss Widdecombe even supported the retention of ancient blasphemy laws. Her black and white views on life seem to me to sum up the way convent school girls were taught to see the world in the sixties and seventies and give you an idea of the social constructs that shaped my early life. Not to mention the strict moral certitudes that would soon tear it apart…

Chapter Five

Moving every couple of years had become a way of life for our family but by this time my parents decided they were going to do things differently. With the arrival of Anna, my mother had the three of us children to look after. My parents recognised that Christine and I had experienced a great deal of disruption to our schooling as a result of following Dad around the world. I was coming to a crucial point in my education, with O-levels looming. I needed continuity. We needed a place we could call home. So my parents bought a house of their own near Bath so that Christine and I could stay at the Convent.

Though they had been married for many years, this was the first house my parents had ever owned. To say it needed 'doing up' is an understatement. It was a near derelict farm cottage. There was no indoor toilet. The bath was at the back of the house in a lean-to shed. Christine and I had to share a room and Anna slept in my parents' room. My father did a great job of decorating, but with no money to renovate, the house facilities stayed as they were. The whole house creaked ominously when anyone walked across the upstairs landing. It was very different indeed to our nice modern house on the RAF station.

I'm not sure I was impressed. It wasn't just that the farm cottage was pretty much falling down, I was disappointed by the neighbourhood too. At the station we'd been surrounded by people. Christine and I could always find a friend to spend time with. Suddenly, we were stuck in a house up a dark unlit single-track road with no neighbours. It was especially isolating for us children. Too young to drive, if our parents couldn't give us a lift to see our old friends, we had to walk 10 minutes to the nearest bus stop and hope that we hadn't just missed one of the few buses a day.

There were some advantages to living close to several farms however, and I made the most of them. I made extra pocket money by picking potatoes and by helping to milk the cows at the weekends. I also learned to ride by exercising horses – a huge, retired shire horse called Lord Snowden at the dairy farm and several others at another farm, a good long walk through the woods. I was a terrible rider though, with no control and one day I ended going up the ramp into a parked removal van because that is where the horse wanted to go. I still loved to be outdoors, but I was starting to be interested in the typical teenage preoccupations. I was very much into music and continued to pore over the pop star posters in Jackie magazine. I also loved *The Champions* which was a new TV series about espionage agents with super-human abilities bestowed upon them. I was mesmerised by the thought that just maybe this could become a future reality.

As I got older, I wanted to be able to go into Bath in the evenings and at weekends but the last bus back to our hamlet left the city shortly after six o'clock. If I wanted to be out any later than that, I had to leave my push bike at a friend's house at the RAF Station where we used to live. The last bus from Bath city centre back to the station left at 23.10. Having picked up my bike I would have to cycle the two miles home, through the woods. This was a little scary at times especially with the owls screeching and couples parked up in their cars but it was also beautiful on a moonlit night. There was no question of me being picked up at the bus stop by my parents, so unless I was looking up at the stars, I just pedalled at speed.

I made the most of every minute I could spend with my friends. School finished at 15.40 but my bus home wasn't until 16.30, leaving me just over half an hour to hang out with the group of teens who had made the bus station their patch. Then I got a Saturday job at Woolworths, which gave me a little more money to spend. I always found ways to earn money to increase my independence.

I was starting to test my autonomy at home. Once, after I argued with Dad, he said that from then on I would have to be in bed at 10pm. This new curfew might have cramped my style but I soon found a way around it. On the first day I was subject to this new rule, I raced home for five minutes to 10. At 10pm, I was tucked up in bed, exactly as Dad had commanded. Five minutes later I got up again and headed for the door.

'Where do you think you're going?' Dad asked, as he saw me leaving the house.

'You told me I had to be in bed at 10,' I said. 'And I was in bed at 10. You didn't say anything about me having to stay there.'

Dad and I were still close. When he was at home, he and I would go to Swindon together to visit the Polish shops there and buy the food he missed from his childhood. Dad loved those trips, which gave him a chance to speak his mother tongue, though I think he was embarrassed that when the shop-keepers addressed me in Polish, they found I couldn't speak a word in reply.

It was on the way back from Swindon that Dad and I had a serious car accident. A lorry jack-knifed in front of us, driving us off the road. I was sitting in the front of the car. By a weird twist of fate, the fact that Dad didn't have his seatbelt on saved his life. He was able to roll away from the worst of the impact. Meanwhile, I was saved because I *was* wearing my seatbelt, still optional then, which stopped me from going through the windscreen.

I escaped the crash relatively unscathed, but Dad broke his femur and had to spend time in hospital. Ironically, while Dad was lying in his hospital bed, with his leg suspended in traction, the overhead hook detached itself, resulting in his leg having to be reset all over again. It never healed well after that, remaining shorter than his other leg and at an unnatural angle. Then, when Dad came home, I sprained my ankle, which meant we ended up on matching crutches. What a pair we made.

On the whole, I wasn't a bad teenager. My acts of rebellion were always silly rather than sinister, such as the times my school friends and I went to the Wimpy Bar in Bath for a burger and swapped the contents of the sugar shaker with the salt. Not very nice for the next person who wanted sugar in their coffee but not exactly serious.

The late sixties was also a time when hippies were reviled by the general public, considered to be a subversive influence on the young. Wearing tie-dye and flares – loon-pants as they were called – my little gang of friends would hang out on the periphery of a big crowd of teenagers and pretend that we were hippies too, shocking passers-by by offering them 'drugs' which were actually only Smarties. We meant no harm by it, though it was probably quite frightening for anyone who wasn't in on the joke.

Real drugs were commonplace in Bath at that time. For the most part I avoided them, though I did smoke a little dope (and dried out banana skins, which were rumoured to get you high but didn't). I was adamant that I would never try LSD or any other psychedelics. I knew that once you swallowed a tab of acid, you had no control whatsoever over the consequences. I saw how it had affected others and I knew that wasn't for me. I hate the feeling of being out of control. The most daring I got was swigging Benylin cough mixture, rumoured at that time to have ingredients that could give you a high. Part of me always remained very conventional.

As I grew up, my dream of being an astronomer evolved. By 15 I was still fascinated by science, but now I specifically wanted to build a nuclear bomb. I was in awe of the technology without a clue about its implications. I think this says a lot about how young and naive I was.

My ambition was to study Nuclear Engineering at Queen Mary's University, London. Dad had slightly different ideas. He wanted me to study at Shrivenham, the Royal Military College of Science. Either way, both Dad and I were very happy with the idea that I would become a scientist.

I chose my O Level subjects accordingly. The convent narrowed down O level choices by making it impossible to study certain combinations. If you wanted to study art and history, for example, you would not be able to study physics and chemistry. The nature of the school meant that we girls were nudged towards art and history. For me, that was all the more reason to choose physics and chemistry.

I was getting to be a little more rebellious at school. Naturally, it being a convent, we had a religious assembly every day. We also had mass once a week. To get out of mass we would hide in the toilets, standing on the pans and lean behind the doors, so that when the nuns came to look for us, they would think the stalls were empty when they peered under the doors. None of the girls in my class wanted to go to mass until a very young priest took over and suddenly everyone wanted to hear the word of God!

My closest friend by this time was a girl called Emma. Emma's parents were getting a divorce and preoccupied as they were with the unravelling of their relationship, they didn't keep so strict an eye on their daughter as my parents kept on me. Emma and I spent much of our spare time together. I'd meet her in Bath most weekends and stayed over at her house. After her parents split, she lived with her father and my parents assumed that he was looking after us, so they were happy for me to stay overnight. On one of those occasions, during the summer of 1970, we went to a gig at the city's university. It was a night that would change my life.

Chapter Six

Emma and I went up to the university expecting nothing more than an evening of good music and perhaps a bit of dancing. We hadn't been there long when I noticed an attractive boy of about our age, who happened to be looking straight back at me. As the band played on stage, we slowly moved closer.

As he approached, I noticed his lovely warm smile and I immediately felt at ease.

'Hi, I'm Tim,' he said.

I smiled back and maintained eye contact, despite feeling rather shy. A moment's pause before I replied, matching him with a simple, 'Hi, I'm Michelle.' I waited, not really sure what to say next. Up until this moment, I hadn't been especially interested in anyone but here I was finding myself immediately physically attracted to Tim and somewhat lost for words.

For a while we just stood there gazing at each other while listening to the band. Eventually, Tim introduced me to his brother Dave and I introduced them both to Emma. I can't say I paid too much attention to Dave or Emma. I was too focused on Tim. He was quite a bit taller than me, very good-looking and fashionably dressed in keeping with the big rock stars of the time, like Paul Rodgers from Free and Robert Plant from Led Zeppelin. I was drawn to his striking brown eyes and long wavy dark hair. It makes me laugh when I remember Emma's mother commenting sometime later, 'He's got the kind of hair that any girl would be proud of.' I don't think she approved.

At the gig, Dave and Emma could see the attraction between Tim and me and they tactfully suggested going to get another round of drinks. On our own, we moved further away so we could hear each other talk.

'Which school do you go to Michelle?' Tim asked. 'I'm in the lower sixth at St Brendan's.'

'I'm at Bath Convent,' I replied. 'Fifth year.' I was pleased to discover that my being a school girl wasn't an issue. Tim, just a year older than me, was much closer in age than I had assumed.

Tim continued, 'I'm doing English, Economics and Greek. I'm applying to university, as I want to be a Child Welfare Officer.'

It sounded interesting but very different to my own plans. I wanted to say something like, 'I hope opposites attract,' but instead I said, 'I'm a scientist at heart so it'll be Maths, Physics and Chemistry at A-level for me,' before adding in a humorous tone, 'I'm told my written work has a lot of room for improvement.'

Tim smiled. 'Like my maths.'

Not long after, Emma and Dave returned with our drinks and our attention went back to the music. Even in that brief conversation, I'd felt a rapport with Tim. He seemed very sophisticated for a 17-year-old. There was just something a bit different about him. Something that made me want to know more.

When the band stopped for a break, Tim suggested that we go for a walk to 'get some air'. Dave and Emma tactfully declined to join us. As we stepped out into the campus grounds, Tim took me by the hand. Though it was cooler outside, I felt hot and my heart was racing. We walked and talked some more.

'Have you got a boyfriend?' Tim asked.

'No,' I said, not daring to ask if he had a girlfriend in return.

'I haven't got a girlfriend,' he said, reading my mind.

We were back at the gig but just as I was about to head back in, Tim stopped me. He put his arms around me and we kissed. It was my very first kiss.

Gentlemen that they were, after the gig ended, Tim and Dave walked me and Emma back to her father's house. It was quite a long way, but we were all too skint to be able to spend money on a taxi or even a bus, and the walk gave me the chance to get to know Tim a little better. Our first kiss at the gig had sealed a potential connection and by the time we reached Emma's door, I knew I had to see him again.

In those days, we had no mobile phones, of course, and though both our families had phones in the house, we'd never have actually called each other up to arrange a date. Instead, Tim and I worked out that at the end of each school day, there would be a short period of time when we were both at the Bath bus station on our way back to our respective homes.

Though, like me, Tim was at a single sex school, he'd already had plenty of experience with girls and I don't think he was looking to 'go steady'. I hadn't really ever thought about it. I wasn't obsessed with boys in the way some girls of my age seemed to be. But soon Tim and I fell into a routine of meeting each other at the bus stop every school day and I found I looked forward to the moment all day long.

The minute the final bell of the afternoon sounded, I would grab my things and walk as quickly as I could to the bus station in Bath. Meanwhile, Tim would get a bus to Bath from his school in Bristol. Between the Bristol bus arriving and my bus back to the hamlet where I lived leaving, we'd have about

20 minutes which we would spend snuggled up in each other's arms. Tim started to refer to me as his 'girlfriend' and I was more than happy to claim him as my 'boyfriend' in return. I liked the way our names sounded linked together when people talked about us. Tim and Michelle. Michelle and Tim.

Those snatched moments after school and at the weekends, brief though they were, quickly became very intense. Was this love? It certainly felt like it to me. At Christmas, six months after we first met, Tim and I exchanged matching friendship rings. They were silver coated in black enamel with an elaborate snake-like pattern on the surface. We wore them every day to remind ourselves and our friends that what we had was serious. Tim became the centre of my world.

Meanwhile my friend Emma started seeing Tim's older brother, Dave. I think in some ways they had been thrown together but they seemed happy enough.

At weekends, we went out as a foursome to local pubs like The Bell, The Packhorse and The Hat and Feathers. The latter was a rather rough pub, often raided by the police looking for drugs. We liked to go there because it was a great place to listen to folk music. The Bell Inn was and still is, an iconic venue for music and The Packhorse, a true country pub. Both were recently saved from closure via community buyouts. The scheme to save The Bell was backed by rock stars Robert Plant and Peter Gabriel.

When we went to these pubs, we didn't get drunk. We didn't have enough money for that. We learned how to make a half pint of scrumpy (the local cider) last for a very long time.

We'd also go for long walks, especially at night. One of our favourite places was Beckford's Tower, a neoclassical folly at the top of Lansdown Hill. The views from the tower were spectacular with the whole of Bath spread out beneath us.

I'd always been a fan of chart music but now that I was with Tim, my tastes shifted again towards rock. I became a big fan of *Free*, whose most famous song *All Right Now*, with its soaring guitars and lyrics made for chanting, would become a real anthem for my generation.

With our Saturday jobs – Tim worked shifts at a petrol station and I was still at Woolworths – we had enough money for some pretty good nights out. Living where we did, we got to see a lot of bands, including some very big names indeed at the Bath Pavilion or Bristol's Colston Hall. We saw *Deep Purple, Curved Air, Pink Floyd, The Who, Fleetwood Mac* and *Jethro Tull*. Rock legends *Led Zeppelin* played the Bath Pavilion in the spring of 1971. I loved their huge hit *Stairway to Heaven*, which would come to mean a great deal to me in later years.

The music of Jimmy Hendrix also featured heavily in the soundtrack of my first summer with Tim. When we heard that Hendrix was going to be headlining at the Isle of Wight festival, Tim and I made a plan to see him play.

'Let's hitchhike down,' suggested Tim.

'Yes!' I replied enthusiastically. 'I've never been to a festival before. Or hitchhiked.'

Tim, sensing I was nervous, took my hand and told me, 'I will look after you, Michelle.'

It was all I needed to hear. I knew I could rely on Tim.

It seemed like a wonderful idea – Tim reassured me that everybody hitchhiked and it wasn't remotely dangerous. However my parents were far from convinced.

'Absolutely not,' was my father's immediate response. 'I won't allow it.'

'Dad, please,' I pleaded. 'Tim will be there and all my friends. I'll be safe.'

But Dad and Mum were adamant. What's more, Dad decided he had to do more than just stop me from going to the festival.

'To be sure you stay home, you're grounded for the whole weekend.'

'That's just so unfair!' I shouted as I stomped off to my bedroom.

I was livid. I knew that festival was one people would talk about for years to come. I couldn't believe how unfair my parents were being, forcing me to miss out on this seminal moment in rock history. So what if I was only 15? It was especially frustrating since Hendrix died of an overdose just a few weeks later.

My parents had met Tim and I'm sure they were impressed by his academic ambitions, but they weren't happy to have him stay over at our house. They were fine with Emma or my other girlfriends, but not any boys. Living as remotely as we did there was also nothing to do, so when Tim came over we ended up spending summer evenings on a grassy track that led from the hamlet where I lived to the nearest village; just hanging around and sometimes smoking dope. On one rare occasion when I did take Tim, Dave, Emma and another friend called Ben back to my house, my father jokingly called out to us: 'Are you going out to take some drugs?'

Of course, he had no idea that he'd hit the nail on the head.

More often than not though, we would meet in Bath and hang out at Emma's house. Her father was too caught up in other things to be bothered about she and I being alone at their place with two boys. At Emma's house, we could do whatever we wanted.

I have absolutely no memory of losing my virginity to Tim or ever having sex with him at all. There's just a vague sense that we first 'went the whole way' outside near *The Packhorse* one early spring evening. Wherever and whenever we had sex, it must have happened. I may have been at a Catholic school but somehow I think an immaculate conception is unlikely.

It's a sad thing, not being able to recall such a momentous occasion as losing one's virginity. I'm sure most people can remember having sex for the very first time. Why I don't remember, I don't know. I don't even have a memory of talking to Emma about it, and I told Emma almost everything back then. Perhaps I've put it from my mind because of the chain of events it set in motion, events too painful to face head on. So I can't tell you how long Tim and I had been seeing each other before we had sex, whether we had sex lots of times or just the once.

The only thing I know for sure is that in the April of 1971, I was pregnant.

Chapter Seven

I sat my O-levels in the May and June of 1971, oblivious to the fact that I was pregnant, or perhaps suppressing the idea because it was simply too frightening to contemplate.

I'm not sure how I could have been unaware of the changes that were happening inside me. I must have noticed that I'd missed a couple of periods, though perhaps I was too preoccupied with my exams to attach much significance to the fact. Pretty much anything could be attributed to the stress of this big moment in my school life.

Since starting to see Tim, my schoolwork had already slipped. Up until that point my Convent school reports had always been glowing with comments like 'Michelle is always so keen', 'she takes a lively interest in everything she does', 'she is a pleasant and cooperative member of the form', 'she is a friendly open girl, always ready to help', 'Michelle's results are very pleasing' and 'her O' level year should be very successful.'

My report summary from December 1970 said, 'Michelle is not always as cooperative as she might be and often displays a negative attitude to school life'. Several of the individual subject teachers had commented on a loss of interest, my carelessness and my general attitude being worrying. As a result, my parents and teachers were on my case. I felt a great deal of pressure to do well so I put my head down and worked harder than I had ever worked, pushing through the tiredness that saw me unable to finish some of the papers I sat.

With my exams out of the way, I had an extra-long summer holiday to look forward to before I would be going back to the Convent to start my A Levels. There were plenty of distractions to be had: nights at the pub, watching bands, parties, even just hanging out in the sunshine.

That summer *The Who* played at the Bath Pavilion. Tim and I were both big fans and we were determined to see them. We queued for more than 10 hours to get tickets. It was not a pleasant experience. It was a very hot day and I didn't feel at all well as we stood in the sun. At one point I felt so ill that I actually lay down on the sticky tarmac. I put my feelings of nausea down to the heat but of course it must have been because I was pregnant.

Other memories from the time also seem different in the light of what happened next. My 16th birthday fell in the summer holidays and I wanted a party. Dad was away with work and though Mum agreed I could have a celebration, she wanted nothing to do with it, telling me only that it couldn't happen at home. With money from my Saturday job at Woolies, I hired the local village hall. There was no social media in those days, but it didn't take long for news of the party to spread far and wide and the small gathering I'd planned was inundated with gate-crashers and quickly got out of hand. In fact, the party got so far out of hand that I left long before it finished.

Tim left with me. As we walked away, I worried about what would happen later.

'What should I do now, Tim? How do I sort this mess out?'

He put his arm around me, reassuring as always.

'We can go back later and clear up. Let's not worry about it now. Let's just have a few moments to ourselves.'

I remember us sitting on a wall, far away from the fray. I felt strangely disconnected from what was going on. It was as though I was watching everything happen on a screen.

Tim walked me back to my house that night and stayed over, along with his friend Ben who'd given up on the party too. For the sake of propriety, the boys couldn't sleep inside the house, so they slept in our wooden garage that was close to falling down. The next day, Mum cooked them breakfast, which was kind and unexpected. As we all sat in the kitchen, I still felt oddly distant from my own life. Perhaps I could sense the coming storm.

My O Level results were mixed. I got the good grades in science I had expected, did better than I hoped in English but failed French. French must have been one of the exams I'd been unable to finish due to the tiredness of my early pregnancy. I returned to school for the beginning of the autumn term – my first as a sixth former. By now I had put on a noticeable amount of weight, to the extent that my parents even joked, 'You're not pregnant are you?' My answer was always 'no!' I was still in denial that I might really be having a baby. The fact that my parents could joke about it suggests that it was the furthest thing from their minds too. They would never have made light of it had they thought it was even a remote possibility.

I threw myself into my A-level studies, working as hard as I could to push through the strange fog of tiredness that had descended over me. All the signs were there, yet each morning I got up and put on my increasingly tight convent school uniform as I had for the past five years. Each day, I continued to play the perfect school girl.

With my tiredness not passing and my increasing weight, Tim and I became concerned that I must be seriously ill. Although I had missed several periods we had not considered, at least not consciously, that I might be having a baby, especially as I had never felt any movement from my growing child. I'm sure that somewhere in the deep recesses of our minds we must have realised it was a strong possibility, neither of us were stupid.

It was Tim who encouraged me to book an appointment at the doctor's surgery on the RAF Station.

'I'm worried about you,' he said.

He came with me. Sitting in front of the GP, with my bump straining the front of my clothes, it must have seemed ridiculous that Tim and I had not concluded I was pregnant. The doctor saw what was going on at once. He didn't need a test.

'Have you considered that you might be pregnant?' he asked.

'No,' I said vehemently, as if the word could make a difference.

The doctor looked up from his notes and gave me a pitying smile.

'Michelle, I'm sending you to the hospital,' he said.

Because I'd not had any antenatal care and I hadn't felt the baby moving, even as far gone as I was, I was taken straight to the Forces hospital at Wroughton in an RAF hospital car. There I was seen by an obstetrician. He spoke to me frankly.

'I look at pregnant women all day long and I can tell you that you are very pregnant indeed.'

As if on cue, I felt my baby move for the very first time. My immediate reaction was panic and then fear. It was October and I was fully seven months pregnant. I had to tell my parents.

I was going to be in so much trouble.

* * *

As with so many things that happened that year, I have only the faintest memory of the moment I told Mum and Dad that I was having a baby. Tim remembers us going first to see the headmistress at Bath Convent. I have no recollection of this at all. I can only imagine what was said to us, based on what Tim's told me and the understanding we had by the time we left. The headmistress was clear, 'You're not to worry. We can sort this out for you.'

That in itself must have been a relief. Here was someone who was going to help us.

'Michelle, you will go to a Catholic mother and baby home and have the baby there. Once the baby is born, he can be adopted by a married couple into a good Catholic family.'

Perhaps I looked astonished by this as she continued, 'Afterwards, you will come home by yourself and we will happily have you back here at school.'

All very simple and matter of fact. I don't imagine I dared to ask for more details. I'd always found the nuns quite scary; certainly they were authoritarian. I would have lacked the courage to question anything I was hearing. Speaking to Tim just recently, he was very clear that, 'there was obviously an established process in place at the convent school for dealing with our situation; like a conveyor belt.'

I must have waited a couple of days after our visits to the GP and to the headmistress to go to my parents, as I struggled to wrap my head around the news and shore up my courage. I know I must have been very anxious as to what their reaction would be. There was very little I feared more than Mum and Dad's disapproval back then.

I think we were in the greenhouse when I eventually dropped the bombshell. Perhaps I chose that location because it was away from the main house, where my younger sisters might be eavesdropping. Perhaps I had in mind that old saying, 'People in glass houses shouldn't throw stones', and thought that the fragile setting would encourage my parents to react in a measured way.

My parents were keen gardeners, who looked to nature for solace when life got tough. The Second World War had had a deep effect on both their psyches. They knew what it was like to face deprivation and starvation, so they grew vegetables, finding a sense of security in the knowledge that they were self-sufficient. Would being surrounded by nature comfort all of us now?

'Mum?' I so needed my mum in that moment. 'Dad? Can I talk to you?'

They turned towards me, eyebrows raised in expectation.

Gathering all my strength, I closed my eyes and whispered, 'I'm pregnant.'

In the silence that followed, I began to wonder if what I'd said had even been heard over the cacophony of bird song in the garden. I waited. A 'pregnant pause' one might say. But slowly I could see that the news had sunk in by the look of horror on both their faces.

'Mum, Dad, I'm sorry,' I said as I burst into tears. 'I'm so, so sorry. I don't know what to do. Please help me.'

Both Dad and Mum remained silent.

Silence was my mother's way of expressing disapproval. It was the things she didn't say that mattered. My father was always more talkative but this time even he was shocked wordless by the news.

My parents were not fiery people but by the time my confession was over, I would have been in no doubt that I was in the deepest of trouble. In their eyes, I had done something unforgivable. At last Mum managed to ask me, 'What are you going to do? You can't have a baby and stay here.'

What could I do? I was seven months pregnant. I was going to have a baby.

Chapter Eight

After that exchange in the greenhouse, things moved quickly. My sisters were not told what was going on. Anna was far too young to understand and Christine needed to be shielded from the unpalatable truth. Presumably my parents also didn't want to risk her letting my terrible secret out of the bag. Christine herself told me recently, 'I had no idea what was going on. I was far too young to be able to comprehend what was happening. All I knew was it was something so bad that I was not allowed to mention it to anyone.'

Over the years I'd learned to read my mother well and I knew Mum's silence had morphed into anger. I remember us standing together at the kitchen sink as I dried the dishes, I could feel her anger radiating towards me like heat from a stove.

'You're nothing more than a slut,' she said as she turned to hand me another plate, her steely eyes meeting mine. There was nothing explosive in the way she spoke but her tone conveyed the extent of her disdain. I looked away, my gaze redirected toward the floor. I felt such shame.

'I'm sorry, Mum,' was all I could say.

Tim had to tell his parents, of course – I wasn't there when he did, just as he hadn't been able to be there with me – and a summit meeting was quickly arranged at my parents' house. I felt a creeping sense of dread as the meeting approached. I'd met Tim's parents a couple of times since we'd been going out, but I didn't really know them and thus I had no idea how they would react to the news that I was carrying their grandchild.

On an afternoon in late October, Tim and his father arrived and Dad showed them into the sitting room as though they were guests invited to the house for an altogether happier occasion. Tim's mother had stayed at home, unable to cope with the situation. The atmosphere was fraught from the start. In retrospect, I think Dad would have preferred not to have Tim or his father in the house at all. Only the chilly autumn weather made it impossible to keep them on the doorstep.

Once in the house, Tim's father sized my parents up. I don't even know if he'd known Dad was Polish and Mum Estonian until they met for the first time. Tim's father was a clerical officer in the civil service. On that day, I perceived he had a very strong, very British sense of class and status, and conveyed a sense of superiority over my 'Eastern European' Mum and Dad, despite Dad's wartime contribution and his role as a commissioned officer in the RAF. It must have been difficult for my parents. Although both had grown up without any sense of class, negative attitudes towards them, individually and as a couple, were not uncommon given their strong foreign accents.

In the early 1970s, a teenage pregnancy was not the sort of thing that happened in good families and, above all, Tim's parents wanted people to know that they were a very good family. They were decent people. They were church goers. Like my father, they were Catholic but they were more serious Catholics in every way. That made the idea of sex outside marriage truly unforgivable for them and they assumed they'd raised their son to think the same. Tim's father acted as though he didn't understand why they had been summoned to my parents' house to discuss something that obviously had nothing to do with them. He couldn't possibly be made to believe that Tim, his perfect, precious, properly-brought-up son would ever get a girl into trouble. I must be trying to trap him.

Then came the most stinging moment of the whole encounter, when Tim's father questioned him, in front of me and Mum and Dad.

'How can you even be sure that this baby is yours?'

I know that question hurt my parents more than anything, containing as it did the implication that I had been sleeping around. Given my parents' history and how important it was to them to be accepted in British society, it must have been particularly hard for them to think of me behaving in such opposition to the social norms of the time. Though they had spent the past few days being furious with me, as soon as Tim's father started casting aspersions, Mum and Dad went to my defence.

'How dare you imply such a thing!' Dad exploded. 'Your son must have led our daughter astray.'

Still Tim's father was adamant and he pressurised Tim to see his point of view.

'Becoming a father while you're still at school will ruin your life,' he said. 'If you insist on being involved in this, we will disown you.'

What a lovely message for parents to give to their son – do the right thing and we will disown you, walk away and you have our blessing. Thankfully, Tim knew that I was carrying his baby and he was ready to take his share of responsibility. Tim always had a very keen sense of responsibility.

If I'd hoped that something good might come of the meeting, I was sadly disappointed. After an hour or so during which angry accusations and blame were batted back and forth across the living room like shuttlecocks, Tim's father decided it was time for them to go. The heated conversation continued out into the garden, down the path and out through the gate to their car. My pregnancy was a hot potato that no-one wanted to be left holding.

As the row persisted all the way to the car, the one thing on which the 'grown-ups' were in agreement was that Tim and I should not be allowed to see each other again and that separation was to start right away. Tim wanted to stay behind with me, to comfort me after the showdown, but his father was insistent that he was going to be leaving with him or he should never come home again.

'Your mother and I want you to walk away,' he told him. 'This is nothing to do with you.'

Their words expressed a wider societal truth that I would quickly come to learn: when a girl got 'into trouble', it was never the boy or the man's fault.

For a moment, Tim hovered between our two families, as though he actually had a choice. But my parents weren't exactly going to invite Tim to come and stay with us. What could he possibly do but go home with his dad, like the child his father thought he was?

As I watched Tim get into the back of his father's car to be driven away, it was as though a part of me was being pulled away with him. We were being ripped apart. I was left behind in enormous distress, sobbing so hard I could hardly breathe. I could see that Tim was distressed too. But I could expect no sympathy from Mum and Dad. Right then, it seemed as though they could hardly bear to look at me. Their anger at the situation had been made far worse by the way Tim's father implied that I was a loose girl who had been badly parented. That was more than Mum and Dad could bear. Though Mum herself had called me a slut, to hear the same words from other people was too much.

Over the next few weeks I would get used to hearing either Mum or Dad say: 'You've made your bed, now you have to lie in it.'

Chapter Nine

In that moment, my life was utterly changed.

It wasn't only Tim that I wouldn't be allowed to see. From that day forward, I was not allowed out of the house. I was taken out of school immediately, cutting short my A-level studies. No work was sent home so that I could keep up with the rest of the class.

The Britain of the early 70s was very different from the Britain of the 40s that my parents had known. In 1969, we'd watched the moon landings. In 1970, the voting age was lowered from 21 to 18. Just that year, 1971, we'd seen pounds, shillings and pence swept away by decimalisation. Yet some things had not changed. Middle class England was still not ready for unmarried mothers.

So determined were my parents that no-one outside the family should know what was going on that I even had to hide away when people came to visit. Fortunately, we didn't have many visitors. My parents were entirely self-sufficient as a couple; wrapped up in each other, they had never needed anyone else. However, one afternoon my father's RAF friend Bill dropped by.

There was panic upon Bill's arrival. As his car pulled up outside the house, I was rushed upstairs to the bedroom I shared with my middle sister Christine. But it wasn't enough for me and my shameful bump to be out of sight. Bill had known me since our days in Singapore and I considered him a sort of uncle. If he'd known I was around, then of course he would have wanted to say 'hello' and find out how I was getting on at school etcetera. There was no way my parents could risk that, so they told me I had to stay silent as well as hidden. Bill simply could not know that I was in the house.

'Bill, hello, what a surprise to see you,' my father's voice drifted up the stairs.

'How are you all? I was nearby, so thought I'd drop in. Hope that's OK?'

It wasn't easy staying quiet in that old cottage, since the bedroom's floorboards creaked at the slightest movement. I could not even go to the bathroom, because that would have meant going downstairs and walking through the room where my father was sitting chatting with Bill as though there was nothing wrong. I just had to sit on my bed with my legs crossed and wait until Bill finally went home, by which time I was desperate for the loo and had to rush to our outside toilet for a pee. The humiliation was immense.

My life as I knew it had come to an abrupt end.

In the farmer's cottage that was our family home, I was entirely isolated. I had been taken out of circulation, like a prisoner in custody awaiting trial; a prisoner who was stuck living with her judge and her jury. I quickly realised that nobody was on my side but day after day, I sat on my bed, not daring to protest. It's amazing what you can come to accept when you feel that you have no choice. Where could I have gone? How long would I have survived on the money from my

Saturday job? To my 15-year-old mind, my parents' word was still law. After a while I even came to believe that perhaps this quasi-imprisonment was what I deserved.

But I could not stay upstairs in my bedroom forever. I was seven months pregnant after all. In a few short weeks, I would be giving birth. My parents could hide me away for now but what would they do when the baby came? From the very beginning, Mum had been adamant. 'You can't stay here with a child.'

As Tim and I had done when we first discovered I was pregnant, Dad had a meeting with the headmistress at Bath Convent. I have a vague memory of being there too, ushered into the convent in secret, wearing my school uniform, Any lingering sense of autonomy had long gone. I was like a parcel being prepared for dispatch.

The headmistress explained the 'problem solving process' to Dad. This sounded like the perfect 'solution' to both sets of parents. Now that the issue of my pregnancy was going to be solved, a degree of civility descended between our parents, phone numbers were exchanged and the plan was put into action.

With all four parents in agreement, the headmistress arranged for me to be sent to a specific 'mother and baby' home in Chepstow, 30 miles away across the Bristol Channel in Monmouthshire. I could live there until my baby was born, far enough away from prying eyes, somewhere where no-one would recognise me.

Sending me away was the only way to save my family's reputation and give me a second chance. No-one need know where I had gone or why. Everything could remain secret. I'd give birth in a hospital far away from anyone who might know our family and my baby would be given up for adoption. I'd come home without a bump, or a child and life would carry on as before. We could say I'd been staying with relatives. These actions were part of the social norm at the time. I was just one of many girls in this position, being carefully and deliberately positioned on the same conveyor belt.

Though we were old enough to be having a baby together, in the eyes of everyone else Tim and I were still very much children. We were not asked at any point how *we* wanted to handle the situation, what *we* wanted to do. Both sets of parents and the school came together determined to make all the decisions for us.

By the middle of November, I was on my way to Wales.

Chapter Ten

The St Anne's Mother and Baby home in Chepstow was run by the Sisters of the Good Shepherd. It was situated in an imposing stucco-fronted house on the edge of the town close to the famous race course.

Dad took me there in the car. Mum didn't come with us. I don't know if she wanted to. She had Christine and Anna to look after. I don't remember anything about the drive or what Dad and I talked about on the way, or even if we spoke at all. I don't even remember having packed for the trip or how I felt about it, though I don't suppose I was thrilled to be sent away from everything I knew. I recall only one moment of my first day at St Anne's with any clarity. I see myself standing on the front porch being greeted by the housekeeper, a dark-haired woman in her thirties, and feeling a sense of relief that she looked OK; like she might be kind. As she welcomed me into the home, I had no idea how the next couple of months would unfold.

Dad came into the house to meet the St Anne's staff. He didn't stay long. As far as I can recall, he didn't come inside any further than the hallway, but I do know he left without giving me any reassurance. There was no hug. No promise that this was for the best and everything would be alright. There were barely any words at all. He acted as though he had just delivered a parcel to the nuns, rather than his terrified eldest daughter. I watched him go, feeling abandoned and rejected. I'd been thrown away. In the eyes of my parents and the church, I had done something so bad that banishment was my just reward. I was a terrible person who had committed a terrible crime. I truly believe I would have been offered more care and compassion had I been a murderer, rather than a teenage girl who'd made a mistake; small and scared of what the future held for her.

After Dad left, I was shown where I would be sleeping and I was introduced to the routine. I understand the nuns who ran the home were from a silent order, but I remember them speaking to us girls and they told us how to use our time to redeem ourselves through work and prayer. The nuns were led by Sister Dolores. She may have been in her thirties but seemed much older, as grown adults do to teenagers. She was very involved in the running of the home. I quickly got the impression that she didn't particularly like me, perhaps feeling I wasn't suitably repentant when I was delivered into her care.

My memories of the home are very sparse, but some things do stand out. We slept in dormitories, maybe four or six to a room. Downstairs there was a large living room and I remember this as having a view over Chepstow Castle. This room had a dining table for 12 or so at one end. I remember sitting at that table with my fellow mothers-to-be for every meal (naturally, we said grace first). I don't remember us being joined by any of the young women who'd already had their babies or ever associating with them, though they must have been around too. Perhaps by keeping us apart, the nuns hoped to keep us new girls safe from the truth about what lay ahead of us in the labour suite. Yet I am sure there was a nursery just off the sitting room and I remember being in the main room with the large table after I had my baby, so maybe we did mix after all. I also have that memory of the young girl who overlapped with me, screaming when her baby was taken away. She had to be physically carried from the home by her parents. I can still hear her now. She was 14 years old.

I remember some of the girls I met in my first few days. Jenny was from Glasgow. She was around 19 or 20, streetwise and very tough compared to the girls I knew from school. She'd grown up in a high-rise block of flats in an area with a reputation for anti-social crime, drugs and little community spirit.

On first acquaintance Jenny seemed quite hard but she was a survivor and underneath the bravado, she had a soft heart. Jenny became the sort of Queen Bee for the rest of us during my time at St Anne's, holding court as we sat at the big dining table day after day.

Penelope could not have been more different to Jenny. Her upbringing was from the other end of the scale. Penelope came from a very well-to-do background and the best word to describe her was 'posh'. Penelope was quite a lot older than me. Her baby was not the result of a sweet teenage romance like mine and Tim's. The father of her baby was a married man, who had no intention of leaving his wife and children. He'd really led Penelope up the garden path. There was no chance of her sad situation ending in a 'happy ever after'.

Eleanor had ended up at St Anne's through similar circumstances to mine. She and her boyfriend, a couple of years older than me, were going steady and very much in love. Their parents thought they were too young to get married and raise a child; they had different ideas.

Chapter Ten

Then there was Mary. Only 18 years old, Mary had come straight to St Anne's from the local prison. I didn't know why she was serving time or whether she would be going back to prison once she'd had her baby – I was too polite and shy to ask – but she seemed nice enough when we chatted to each other in the sitting/dining room.

We were an eclectic bunch, we St Anne's girls. Pretty much the only thing we had in common was that we were all having babies out of wedlock. Although I was used to making new friends, I found it hard to do so here. I'm not sure why. Maybe our own desperate and sad situations weighted each of us down too much. For me, this meant that although I was always with other people, I felt isolated and desperately lonely.

St Anne's was no hotel. Though the local authority and, in some cases, parents were paying for us to be looked after by the staff there, we were still expected to earn our keep. There were always household chores to be done. Though I don't remember being asked to cook, I did spend a lot of time in the large kitchen, under the watchful eye of one of the nuns, cleaning the surfaces and scrubbing the floor. I sometimes wonder if it was all part of a strategy to make us feel we were doing penance for our sin. We were certainly compliant, as not one of us would challenge what was asked of us.

We helped each other to do most of the tasks but scrubbing the floor was a chore that we all vied to take on in the final month of our pregnancies, thinking that it would bring labour about. I don't know where we got that idea from but it was taken as fact.

When the housework was done, we were set to gainful employment. The nuns had set up a clever little business, ideal for pregnant girls: packing hair pins. Each morning after our chores, we mums-to-be would sit around the big table in the dining room, counting hair pins from a big box into smaller individual packets, so they could be sent to the shops. Jenny would usually sit at the head of the table, and though we were not encouraged to talk, she would regale us with stories from her life in Scotland, so different from my own. I listened to her avidly, fascinated by her experiences and in admiration of her handling of the challenges in her life.

Occasionally, in the afternoons, we would leave the confines of the home and its gardens to walk into the town. We all longed to be away from St Anne's and feel part of the real world for a while, but a trip into the centre of Chepstow was not the pleasant experience we might have hoped for. The home was clearly notorious amongst the locals and their stares and whispers followed us through the streets. We were 'those girls' from 'that place'. We were all of us pretty used to disapproval by this point, but the unkind judgement of those strangers was still hard to take. It was as though they thought our very presence might corrupt the local youngsters. It definitely took the fun out of an afternoon in town.

Back at the home, it was supper at the big table then 'lights out' fairly early. One of the stronger memories I have of that time is that before turning in we would kneel by our beds in prayer, while one of the nuns stood over us. We'd thank God that we were being looked after and ask for his forgiveness. I remember holding my rosary beads while we said endless Hail Marys and the Lord's Prayer; my head bowed in shame and me full of contrition for being such a terrible sinner. On Sundays and several other days in the week I also attended mass and went to confession with Father Hall in the home's chapel. 'Bless me father for I have sinned' was a constant theme in my life. I didn't mind all those prayers at the time. I went compliantly through the daily routine: prayers, chores, chores, prayers. I felt I had a lot of penance to do.

Chapter Ten

I don't remember if in the darkness of the dormitory at night we ever talked about what was going to happen to our babies, but the mantra I sensed around the home for the majority was that we were sinners and going to do the 'right thing' or the 'best thing' for our unborn children – and that meant giving them away.

Chapter Eleven

Girls at St Anne's were allowed to have visitors but visits from our babies' fathers were few and far between. In all the time that I was there, I remember only two boyfriends visiting: Eleanor's and my own. Tim.

Defying his parents' wishes, Tim came to see me as often as he could. At weekends, if he wasn't working at the petrol station, he would catch the bus from Bristol to Chepstow, often with Emma. Sometimes he would come with his brother Dave and we would walk to the ruins of Chepstow Castle, just as we used to walk up to Beckford Tower to see the view in less complicated times. When Tim couldn't visit, he would call me on the phone which hung on the wall in a small booth in the corridor outside the sitting room. Seeing Tim and getting those calls was very comforting.

Abandonment was a regular theme of our conversations at the long table where we ate our meals and packed those pins. That Tim was standing by me made me feel a little better about my situation. I hadn't just been used and cast aside. It proved that what Tim and I had was real love. It also gave me hope.

One day, shortly after Eleanor's baby was born, there was a huge commotion downstairs in the hallway. Her boyfriend had arrived, determined to take both of them away, pushing back against the process of what was expected of them. It was so good to see this! I relayed this story to Tim with great excitement. I hope things worked out for them in the end.

Most of all, I was lonely. On one occasion, Tim tried to help me cement some friendships, taking me and three other girls out to the pub for a drink. It was November, bitterly cold outside and the only place where we could go that was warm. Unfortunately, the nuns were informed and they were not impressed, telling me I was bringing St Anne's into disrepute. I was in big trouble and I'm not sure it brought me closer to anyone.

My parents visited too. Whenever they came, I was quickly loaded into Dad's car and we'd drive to a motorway service station near to the Severn Bridge for a cup of tea. These were uncomfortable outings. Mum was never relaxed and was always looking over her shoulder, nervous as she was that even in this anonymous place miles from home, someone who knew our family might see us all together and discover my terrible secret. And every time the conversation was the same. Mum would ask, 'Have you decided what you're going to do yet?'

I would say nothing, knowing what was coming next.

'You're not coming home with a baby, Michelle. It has to be adoption. Otherwise you are out there on your own.'

She would pause for a while as if expecting me to answer, then meet my silence with, 'Well?'

I never knew what to say. I knew what was expected of me. I needed to give up my baby so that we could all go back to pretending we were good, upstanding people who didn't make this kind of mistake. Mum was like a dog with a bone. I would look over to Dad, my eyes pleading for his support. More often than not, I would be met with complicity by his silence.

However on one occasion, Mum was so hard on me that Dad actually stepped in.

'Give her a break,' he said.

I don't know who was more surprised – me or my mum – but I'm pleased to say it stopped her in her tracks. All the same, I was glad when they loaded me back into the car and took me back to Chepstow.

With my baby not due until January, I found myself stuck in St Anne's over Christmas 1971. Tim called me on Christmas Eve. He was on a shift at the petrol station but told me that he would be going out with his friends – our friends – after work. As he outlined his plans for a fun night on the town, I began to feel more and more angry.

'You're going out?'

'It's just a few drinks.'

All I could think was how unfair it was that Tim would be celebrating Christmas in the pub while I was stuck at St Anne's with the nuns. He'd be toasting the season with many of our friends (none of whom knew of my situation) while I would be kneeling by my bed to say prayers for forgiveness. It struck me then that even though the baby I was carrying was half Tim's, I was the only one being made to pay for our 'sin'. I was the one who'd had to leave home and come to this place that was pretty much a prison. I was the one who had been torn away from my family and friends. I was the one who'd had to leave school and abandon my university plans. Who knew if I would ever go back? From my perspective, Tim's life was carrying on pretty much as normal. The wave that had left me floundering had simply washed over him, leaving almost nothing changed. He was still going to school, doing his Saturday job, seeing our friends… So I didn't want to hear about his big night out.

I'd be damned if Tim was going to go out and have fun while I had to stay in and say Hail Marys. I was full of resentment. Why should he be able to enjoy himself? That evening, I kept him on the phone for as long as I possibly could, making sure he knew just how unhappy I was, hoping that if I just kept telling him how awful things were, then he would be forced to recognise how terrible things were for me compared to him. I wanted him to feel as bad as I did, sitting there in the cold booth on that pay phone. I wanted him to have a miserable Christmas Eve too. At that moment, as far as I was concerned, it was the least he deserved.

'Don't go, Tim. I need you to talk to me. I'm having such a horrible time.'

It didn't work of course. Tim still went out without me.

But the festive season did not go entirely unmarked at St Anne's. No matter how grim our circumstances, my fellow mums-to-be and I still found small opportunities for fun and laughter.

On New Year's Eve, those of us who were yet to have our babies had a little bit of a party to welcome in 1972. We played music and, even though I was just days from my due date, I got up and danced with abandon. I was enjoying myself so much that one of the nuns was dispatched to tell me to simmer down. I didn't care. That night I was just like any other 16-year-old girl. The confident and carefree child I had once been shone through for a couple of hours. It felt as though the new year could signal a bright new beginning, even for someone who had really messed up; a bad girl; someone like me.

Chapter Twelve

On New Year's Eve 1971, I don't think I had any idea how much things would change for me over the next few short weeks. As we rang in 1972, it still seemed possible that I would be able to give birth, hand my baby over for adoption and slip straight back into my previous life, with no long-term damage done. I would be redeemed and my child would have parents who were fit and proper, unlike me.

I was completely clueless with regard as to how my pregnancy was progressing. We all were. It goes without saying that I'd had very little in the way of sex education at the Convent – as far as I recall it was limited to reproduction in frogs. As mums-to-be we were taken to the Lydia Beynon Maternity hospital for regular medical checks; a grand hospital building, that had once been home to a wealthy coal baron in Newport. My recollection is there was no such thing as ante-natal classes for us. We were the bad girls and needed to be kept away from the respectable local married mothers. Certainly, no-one told me what to expect while I was expecting. Just like when I faced my eye operation aged 10, I had absolutely no sense of what lay ahead.

Chapter Twelve

We were driven to our appointments at the hospital in an ambulance. As well as routine check-ups, I had to go to Newport on a number of occasions to have my blood pressure taken and be checked for signs of pre-eclampsia. If you were the only one the ambulance driver was picking up on any particular day, he would let you sit up front. The driver seemed to know a great deal more about pregnancy than I did and he told me, while bringing me back to the home one day, that he was sure I would have my baby in the middle of the night.

'You all do,' he said with certainty. 'And I'll be there to take you to Newport when it happens.'

He was right.

I was very grateful that the friendly driver was working when I went into labour in the early hours, exactly as he had predicted. He was a very kind man, probably in his fifties, who didn't seem in the least bit judgemental of me or my situation. Sitting beside him in the cab of the ambulance was comforting as I headed towards the big unknown. Strange as it sounds, that ride to the hospital stands out as an oddly happy memory from what would be a very difficult time. For a short while, I could pretend that I had a real friend by my side with me.

Thanks to the lack of preparatory ante-natal classes, I had no clue how my labour would unfold. After the ambulance driver delivered me to the maternity suite, I was suddenly on my own again. What was going happen to me? Last time I had been in hospital as an inpatient I had been held down so that whatever was necessary could be done to me. I wonder if, despite my having no conscious memory of that time, it made things worse for me now?

I was scared and in pain as my contractions grew stronger and closer together. Was it supposed to hurt so much? I felt sure that my baby would burst from me at any moment. I have a memory of being in a toilet cubicle when my waters broke, though I can't be sure whether that happened at the hospital or back at St Anne's. Either way, it was a shock that left me scared and embarrassed. No-one had told me my waters would break.

In the maternity suite itself, I was prepared for the birth in the most terrible way. I had absolutely no idea that my pubic hair would be shaved off, or that I would be given an enema. No-one had ever mentioned it. The experience was horrible and undignified.

I had never felt so alone as I did while I waited to give birth that January night. While the hospital was full of people, there was no-one I could turn to. No-one to hold my hand and reassure me that everything I was going through was perfectly normal and the baby and I would be OK. There was no-one to say, 'I'm here for you.' I was heading into a dark tunnel with no sight of what was going to happen next. I was terrified, all alone and totally unprepared, with no-one at my side to comfort me, encourage me, or even just hug me.

Since I'd gone into labour in the middle of the night, there was no way for me even to get a message to Tim. I would not have dared to ask someone to call him at his parents' house, not at such a late hour. Instead, I cursed him loudly as the contractions grew more frequent and harder to bear. Why was I having to go through this pain alone? What had I done to deserve this? Suddenly, all those prayers I'd said on my knees at bedtime seemed like a cruel joke. No-one had been listening.

Chapter Thirteen

My labour was managed by a female midwife. I cannot see her in my mind's eye but I remember her as kind, professional and efficient as she went about her work. She did her best to keep me calm and relaxed, but I was too scared to be very compliant.

Pain relief was much more basic in the 1970s than it is now. The only thing on offer was 'gas and air'. There was no chance of an epidural. I took the gas and air but I could still only get through the ordeal by shouting out loudly. Repeatedly I cried out 'TIM!' at the top of my voice in a harsh and angry tone, my cries increasing in their intensity and duration as my labour progressed. Somehow, cussing Tim seemed to make the pain of each contraction a little easier to bear. I was quite dramatic. There were times when I begged and pleaded with the midwife to end my ordeal, screaming:

'Make it stop. I don't want to do this', grabbing her by her arm when I could reach to make sure I had her full attention.

'Please stop this NOW, please help me.'

As if there were any way to bring my labour to an end without my giving birth. The midwife calmly did her best to bring me back to reality.

'Michelle, nothing is going to stop this from happening now, your baby is on its way.'

I was terrified.

Later, the midwife would tell me that my language and requests for the impossible had kept the whole team amused. I was the most colourful patient she'd ever had to deal with.

I worked as hard as I could to do as the midwife told me and give birth without intervention but at a certain point during the labour, it was decided that I would have to have an episiotomy to enlarge the opening for the baby to get through. I don't know whether it was necessary for my baby's safety or whether the hospital just wanted to speed up my labour and get me through the maternity suite in as little time as possible. The procedure was done by a male member of the medical team, possibly an obstetrician. He was brisk and business-like, coming into the room only to make the painful incision before letting the midwife take over again.

I was in labour for five hours. Five hours of pushing and crying and shouting out like never before. After one final push, my baby was born at 6.30 in the morning on the 13th of January. He was a boy, weighing 7lb and 2oz, and he was perfect.

While the medical team checked my baby over, the midwife turned her attention to me.

'You're all done, Michelle. Off you go back to the ward.'

Used to doing exactly what I'd been told to do, I quickly tried to get up, despite how weary and dazed I felt. The midwife was horrified.

'No, no,' she cried. 'Lay back down. I was joking. You need to stay in bed.'

A few minutes later, she handed me my son, washed and swaddled in a hospital blanket.

I already knew that I would be calling him Timothy Peter, after his father and with the English form of Piotr, from my own heritage. As I got my first proper look at my baby's face in the cool morning light, I was satisfied that the name would fit.

'Hello, Tim,' I murmured.

Though I had carried Baby Tim for nine months, the moment of meeting him face-to-face at last still came as a big surprise. My feelings for him were immediate and full-on. I was flooded with love as I gazed upon the face of the little human before me. This little human that Tim and I had made. He was so tiny and yet he already filled my heart.

As Baby Tim lay in my arms, and I basked in this unexpected rush of happiness after all the pain, one of the nurses came over and looked me deep in the eyes.

'How on earth could you give him up now?' She asked.

The nurse's question was meant with kindness, I have no doubt. She knew I had come to the hospital from St Anne's and what was likely to happen next. Perhaps, looking back now, she was trying to let me know that despite everything I'd been told, at that moment, I still had a choice. Baby Tim and I could stay together. I still had the chance to be a proper mum.

Chapter Fourteen

Not long after my baby was born, the doctor who had performed the episiotomy returned to stitch it shut again. Again, I only have only the vaguest of memories but I remember a man with dark hair, in a white coat, who barely spoke to me. I didn't get a sense of compassion as he wordlessly performed his task.

I can't help but wonder if he treated all new mothers in the same way or if there was so little communication between us because of my status as a St Anne's girl. Afterwards, I was given an orange rubber ring without which I would not have been able to sit down for the pain. Perhaps the practice of giving episiotomies was widespread, but I remember noticing a couple of other young girls from St Anne's carrying those rings wherever they went; maybe I noticed them because they were known to me and we tended to sit together for meals, or maybe not. Now that I think of it, I also remember how us girls from St Anne's would walk down the hospital corridor between the bays with our heads held down, avoiding any eye contact with the other mothers. We all felt so much shame.

I was taken from the maternity suite to a ward, while Baby Tim was taken to the nursery. I was still in a daze, but the ordeal of labour was already fading into a strange sort of dream. A couple of hours earlier I'd thought the contractions would never stop. Now I lay my hands on my empty belly. Had I really just had a baby?

Later on that first day, Tim would meet our child for the first time. The civility between our parents meant that a message had been passed from my dad to his and on to Tim at school. The moment he heard Baby Tim had been born, Tim was on his way. In my head, I have a vague image of him, still wearing his school uniform, holding his son with some bemusement. Perhaps, because Tim wasn't the one who had been pregnant for nine months, it still felt like a weird dream to him. He himself says he was in a state of total shock.

Tim's sense of responsibility was still as strong as ever. I was in the ward without any money and before Tim left, he gave me all he had. This left him penniless, even without bus fare to get home. Thankfully he was in his school uniform and although it was not valid for the journey from Newport, the driver let him onto the bus with his school bus pass.

Nowadays, new mothers are on their way home with their babies hours after giving birth, but in the 1970s, it was common practice for mothers and their new-borns to remain in hospital for as long as 10 days. Although the hospital staff knew I was not going to be keeping my child, I was still expected to have that 10-day stay. I was given a bed in a bay that could accommodate four or maybe six. I had the spot nearest the window. Across the ward, in the furthest corner from me, was another new mum. Beyond that fact, her circumstances could not have been more different from mine. She was married. I don't remember her name, but let's call her Laura.

Laura had not had an easy journey to motherhood. I would learn that after 11 years of trying and a series of miscarriages, she'd had to fight hard to bring her first baby to full term, injecting herself every day with drugs to help her maintain her pregnancy. Thus, when her baby was born, it was an occasion for double, treble or even quadruple the usual amount of joy. Her bed was surrounded by flowers and she had a constant stream of visitors. Laura's husband clearly doted on her. He would visit every day, arriving the moment visiting hours began and staying until the very end. He brought fresh flowers or fruit every time he came. Their joy, their hope and delight would emanate from their side of the ward. There was no doubt that the birth of her child was a source of great happiness for everyone who knew and loved her. It was a celebration of the new life she had brought into this world.

Meanwhile, I sat alone in my bay. There were no flowers for me. No thoughtful gifts. No sounds of joy or celebration, no cards of congratulation. Tim was unable to visit again and I think my parents came to visit only once, if at all.

I felt desperately lonely as I watched the stream of people who came to gaze at Laura's baby.

Everyone saw her baby's birth as a blessing. Her baby was a miracle. My own beautiful child was still variously an embarrassment, a source of shame, and a problem yet to be solved. I was filled with deep sadness as I listened to the happy chatter and joy around Laura's bed. I held my baby close, with so much love – it was us against the world – yet the juxtaposition of our very different worlds reinforced what a terrible person I was. I was worthless as a mum. I deserved all this pain and the shame.

One of the nurses used to do her best to help by coming to talk to me for a few minutes whenever she was on shift. Otherwise, I was on my own, lost in my own world. I remember on around day three or four, sobbing my heart out, probably a combination of everyday baby blues kicking in, heightened by my particular circumstances.

Chapter Fourteen

I'm sure that Laura and her husband must have known my situation. I was sure that everyone did. As I walked the hospital corridors on my way to the bathroom or the dining room, I was aware that many of the people I passed would suddenly fall silent and stare. It was just as it had been when I went into town in Chepstow with my friends from St Anne's. I might as well have had a big 'U' for unmarried mother on my forehead or rung a bell to announce that I was coming so that people could get out of my way.

There was no reason why this respectable married couple shouldn't have been just as scandalised by my presence as everyone else in that hospital. But if they were, they didn't show it.

One day, as visiting time drew to a close – possibly after seeing me so emotional – Laura's husband did something quite unexpected; he came over to 'visit me'. He sat by my bed.

'Hello,' he said. 'How are you and your baby doing? What's he called?'

'This is Tim,' I said. 'And he's doing really well.'

I was somewhat taken aback by my visitor. He leaned in to take a closer look.

'Gosh, what a gorgeous boy. You must be very proud.'

It meant so much to me to hear these words and feel treated like a normal mum. He made me think that perhaps I wasn't such a bad person after all. Then, to my surprise, his visit turned into a routine. Every day with five minutes to go before the end of visiting hour, Laura's husband would cross the ward to talk to me.

'How are you, Michelle? And how's Tim doing today?'

I could see he took delight in hearing about me and in the tiny changes I was noticing in my baby day-by-day.

'May I hold him, please?' he would ask before gently cradling Baby Tim in his arms. I loved seeing this as, just for a moment, I could imagine this kind man as the doting grand-parent I wished my father would be.

For these brief moments every day my corner of the bay was filled with me sharing the joy of my son with another and feeling cared for too. It was a gesture of such kindness that thinking about it still fills me with so much emotion. That lovely, gentle man could have stayed wrapped up in his own happiness but he – and obviously Laura too – had noticed my despair and reached out to me. They'd asked themselves what they could do.

When it was time for Laura – this lovely lady – to take her baby home, she made sure that her husband brought the flowers that had surrounded her bed over to mine. They left me their chocolates too. For a couple of days I could pretend that the flowers had been bought for me and that I was every bit as loved and cherished as the other mums on the ward.

Fifty years later every cell in my body still responds to the memory of that couple's extraordinary empathy. Thinking about them brings bucket loads of tears to my eyes. I wish that I knew who they were, so that I could thank them for making one of the darkest moments of my life a little bit easier to bear. Whenever I think of them I can feel their compassion and kindness wrap itself around me.

Chapter Fifteen

At the end of my 10 day stay in hospital, I returned to the mother and baby home by ambulance with Baby Tim in my arms. Because of the way adoption worked at the time (at least, because of the way I *thought* it worked), after Baby Tim's birth, I was to be given a six-week long period to consider my options. I couldn't spend those six weeks at home with Mum and Dad (Mum had made that very clear), so I had to spend them back with the nuns at St Anne's.

What happened next is a mystery. I'm sure that I must have been expected to look after my baby, yet I have no memory of the precious moments of our time together. I feel so very sad about that. I have a vague sense that in the dormitory I was moved to upon my return from hospital, there was a crib by the side of each bed. Is that where Baby Tim slept? I don't remember feeding him, changing him or bathing him (though I am sure I was taught how to bathe him during my time in the hospital). And what about nappies? In the 1970s there was no such thing as a disposable nappy. Instead, we had to use heavy terry cloth squares, fastened in place with a large pin. For some reason I only remember the pins and having to push the cap into a safety position. I don't imagine St Anne's sent that particular laundry burden out. We must have washed the nappies ourselves.

As strange as it sounds, I don't even know if I breast-fed Baby Tim during the first few weeks of his life. I probably didn't. At the time of his birth, it was common practice to prevent unmarried mothers whose babies were ear-marked for adoption from lactating, with an injection of powerful chemicals that have since been linked to a variety of illnesses including cancer. Was I given that injection? I'm not sure, but it seems likely that I was. I was probably told that bottle-feeding Baby Tim from the start would make it easier for his adoptive family to take over. Likewise, cutting off lactation as soon as possible would make it easier to keep the birth of my baby a secret when I got back home to Bath. The shame surrounding having a child outside marriage was such that of course it was expected I would be denying it had ever happened.

Fifty years on, I'm still trying to find a way to piece the memories back together. I must have held my baby close, hugged him with tenderness and love, talked to him and marvelled over his tiny fingers and toes, yet I can't bring to mind a single picture of that time – much as I want to. All those precious moments that we shared as mother and son, the only time in my life when I was his MUM. All that love and that sense of belonging together. These are the memories that I want back so much. Instead, all I have are a few photos that are now yellowing with age.

The one thing I do know is that at some point during the weeks I spent at St Anne's after Baby Tim's birth, it was decided that he should be christened. I don't think I would have chosen to have him baptised, but I imagine it was a requirement for babies staying in a Catholic mother and baby home and I would have complied. Thanks to my upbringing, I was still very compliant from a religious point of view. Indeed, one nun remarked to Tim what a good Catholic I was, going to mass every day!

Everything I know of that day is thanks to the fact that someone took the time to take photographs. When I look at them, no memories come back to me, but I see the photos, I know I am there. I can see it's my son's christening. Baby Tim is dressed in a long white christening gown that must have been provided by the nuns. In one picture, he is lying on a sumptuous white satin and lace pillow, gazing up at whoever was taking the photograph. He looks happy and healthy, every bit the cherished infant he was.

Tim came to Chepstow for the occasion. One of the photographs captures us together with our son. We are wearing similar outfits; a detail which we must have coordinated ahead of time. My dress matches his shirt, both a purple snakeskin print. I've pulled my hair up into a neat bun, accented with ringlets around my hairline. I've done my make-up carefully, in honour of the significance of the day. Tim's thick dark hair is long and loose. We make a beautiful couple; a beautiful young family. Our friendship rings are visible in the photograph too, only now they sit on the finger signifying marriage. I have no idea if we had decided to do this on that day, or if I had been wearing my ring in this way to try and lessen my shame in public. Tim stands behind me, and I lean into him with my baby – our baby – in my arms. My eyes are closed and happiness radiates from my face and I am beaming. Mine is the face of a proud young mother. You can see my joy and my love for my son. In that moment, I was everything a good mum needs to be.

Among the other guests at the baptism were Emma and Tim's brother Dave, who had both been such good friends to me all through my time at St Anne's. Emma was dressed from head to toe in black and sported a large crucifix, which must have worried the nuns. She looks a little awkward as she stands beside me in one photograph. A good Convent girl, Emma was probably as intimidated by the nuns as I was. It's easy to forget that we were all still in our teens.

Perhaps surprisingly, my father and my little sister Christine were also in attendance. A photograph shows Christine, who must have been around 12, holding Baby Tim in her lap. She's wearing her school uniform but she looks delighted to be meeting her nephew and not at all nervous at having such a precious bundle in her care. You can tell that she would have loved to be taking Baby Tim back to Bath. What a good auntie she would have been.

Mum was not there. Whether that was because she had to stay home with Anna or because she didn't approve or want to be there, I don't know. But Dad did make the journey that day and he brought with him a christening gift, just like any other proud grandparent. It was a cutlery set comprising a spoon, knife and fork. The set was gold-plated; not a cheap gift but a properly thought-out one, that Baby Tim was meant to keep for his whole life. I wonder what became of it? Did it go with my baby to his adoptive home? Did his adoptive parents keep it for him or throw it away?

There were other gifts too. Tim's mother, who, like mine, had decided not to come to the baptism, had sent a little woollen outfit she'd made specially. I wonder what went through her mind as she knitted that tiny layette in soft baby wool. Tim said that after that awful meeting between his father and my parents in October 1971, his parents had refused even to mention my pregnancy. Yet the knitted outfit proves that Tim's mother must have been thinking about it. Did she feel any sadness as she thought of the grandson she would never see? Did she feel guilty? Or was it just a way for her to alleviate her guilt, while still feeling relieved that Tim and I were on the conveyor belt process to adoption?

When my baby was born, he had four living grandparents. He had several aunts and uncles. He had godparents in Emma and Dave. Did it ever occur to Tim's mother that she and her husband could have stepped in to help keep Baby Tim in the family? What was going through my dad's mind as he posed for photographs, looking pleased as punch to have a grandchild? Why didn't he put his foot down and insist his grandchild came home with me? Looking at the photographs 50 years on, I still search all the faces for answers.

Baby Tim's baptism took place on February 4th. Our last day together came just 10 days later: February 14th, 1972, Valentine's Day.

Yet again, my memories of that day are unclear. Who bathed and dressed Baby Tim on the day we were parted? Was it me? Reading accounts of other women who relinquished their babies in similar circumstances, I wonder whether I had made or bought a special set of clothes for this most significant and terrible moment. I must at least have kissed him as I placed him in his crib.

My memory of this time is part visual and part kinaesthetic. I do remember the sun pouring in through the nursery windows as I sneaked downstairs to look at him one last time. When I think about it, I can feel my heart almost being crushed from the emotional pain, not only in my chest but throughout my whole body, as it must have done that day. Though the adoption wasn't yet a done deal, something in me must have been sure that I would never see him again.

I left the mother and baby home myself that same afternoon. I no longer had a baby, ergo I was no longer a mother.

There was no reason for me to be at St Anne's any more. No doubt someone else was waiting for my place in the dormitory.

My journey back to Bath was very different from the journey I'd taken in the opposite direction. I have a strong memory of taking a bus between Chepstow and Bristol, staring out at the grey water as I crossed the Severn Bridge.

I hate that I had to make that most important journey alone. Perhaps I thought I wanted to, but looking back I am heartbroken for the young woman that I was, still only 16 years old, bearing so much sadness entirely on my own. I was in such a vulnerable state. My hormones must have been all over the place too.

It's an odd memory as I cannot imagine that my parents would not have collected me. If I had gone home under my own steam, I would have had my luggage with me and have had about ¾ mile to walk from the bus stop to my parents' house. That would have been too much, not to mention an opportunity for people to see me or talk to me. Given that things had to be kept secret, logic tells me that I would have been collected by my father. Maybe he picked me up from the bus station in Bath.

But perhaps I was allowed to make my own way home because my welfare no longer mattered to the nuns, or the social workers. My baby was safely placed with a foster family. An adoption agency in Bristol would soon find him a permanent home. I'd played my part and now I was completely irrelevant. I'd been cast aside.

There was no-one there for me, nowhere I could go but home and nowhere for my grief to be shown or shared. I was falling into an abyss while 'knowing' it was what I deserved. Leaving my baby was supposed to be the first step on the road back to respectability. For so long afterwards that meant never shedding a tear in view of anyone else, never sharing my grief or really understanding what and how I felt. In order to be a respectable single woman in society I would need to live a lie. Nobody could ever know I had been a 'bad girl'. Although Baby Tim's existence was to be a secret, inside I also knew I was transitioning into a second category of shame – I was a mother who gave her child away.

We must remember that in everyone's eyes, I was just one of 'those women' who dared to get pregnant outside marriage. I had sinned, not just against God and in the eyes of the Church, but against my family and society as a whole. I deserved everything I got and I needed to feel ashamed. I needed to be punished.

And the saddest part of all? Back then I believed that too.

Chapter Sixteen

There was no comfort to be found at home. Though my parents had let me come back (without my baby, as was always the condition), and they wanted anyone looking in from the outside to think that everything was normal again, they were clearly still angry with me and the atmosphere in the house was frosty from the start. There was no kindness or sympathy. They didn't want to know about my sadness. They stuck to the line, 'You've made your bed. You've got to lie in it.'

I was at home under sufferance and I should think myself lucky that I hadn't been cast out on the street. I later learned that in my parents' eyes my having a baby was such a serious misdemeanour that while I was at St Anne's, they'd rewritten their will, reducing the percentage of their estate that would come to me after they died from an equal third with my two sisters to something smaller that more accurately reflected my state of disgrace. It was meant to hurt when they told me – and it did.

For the most part, my memories of those early months of 1972 back at my parents' cottage are jumbled and unclear. In theory, I could still change my mind about the adoption as I had yet to sign the papers that would make adoption irrevocable. I remember my mother barely speaking to me except to ask the eternal question. 'Have you made your decision yet?' To her mind, there was still only one correct answer. I also remember one other moment in sharp, filmic detail, the seismic moment when it was finally decided that Baby Tim was going to be adopted.

It was the middle of March. Tim and I were sitting side by side on the swings in the children's playground on the RAF Station – still barely more than children ourselves. It was empty apart from us. Tim turned towards me.

'So it's definitely adoption then.'

His words were a gut punch, signifying that we had come to the end of our deliberations. It was clear to me then that even if we wanted to, we couldn't go any further forward without support from our parents, the Church or the State. No-one was there for us in any capacity. We were at the end of the road. My silence indicated my acceptance.

Later that day, alone in the bedroom I still shared with my younger sister, I was beside myself. In order to contain any signs of how I was feeling around my parents, as expected, I knew had to get out. I had to express my pain.

Though it was only early evening, it was already dark. It was a wet night and the wind was blowing a gale. The weather could not have reflected my mood more perfectly. I remember walking along the side of an A road, a fast road, with no street-lights and no pavement on either side. I walked into the wind, crying hard, not taking care, not paying attention. Cars whizzed by, closer and faster than they should have been. Any one might have knocked me off my feet. Any one might have ended my life in a second. I was so dazed, so devastated, that my chance to be Baby Tim's mother had finally run out that I was oblivious to the danger.

It was done. The decision to give my child up for adoption had been made. I was overwhelmed by grief that crashed over me like waves in a storm. I was glad to be alone, alone in the rain. I needed time to absorb the enormity of what was going to happen. I wanted the rain to wash away my despair. I would have walked all night or to the ends of the earth if it would have made a difference.

What happened next? Who knows?

The days after that conversation in the playground are a blank. My brain did its best to protect me, refusing to hold on to the bleak feelings of desolation that must have followed our momentous choice. I must have told Mum and Dad what Tim and I had decided. Someone must have spoken to the school or St Annes's or to the social worker. Whatever path was taken, it led to the adoption agency looking for a permanent family for my baby. I'm sure all four parents felt a sense of gushing relief, that the 'problem' was going to be solved just as they had planned, while I turned in on myself, full of shame and confusion.

I'd had a baby outside marriage. That made me one kind of bad mother. Now I was agreeing to adoption. That made me the very worst kind of mother there was; a mother who gave her baby away. Whichever way I turned, whatever I did, in this circular loop, one thing was certain – I was unfit to be a mum. And from that moment onwards, with my parents and with the outside world, I was expected to pretend that I had never had a baby. I did not have a son.

'You are young. You can have other children. Remember this is best for baby (never *your* baby). You're doing the right thing… Now you can get on with your life'.

Chapter Sixteen

All those empty words had been said to me at some point; not sure when or by whom, but how stupid people were to think for one second that any of it was true.

Chapter Seventeen

I had left St Anne's in mid-February but I didn't go back to school at once. Instead, it was decided that I would re-join the lower sixth after Easter, at the beginning of the summer term. In the meantime, I had to stay at home and help about the house. It was probably for the best. I had a great deal to process in those weeks.

By this time, my relationship with Tim was utterly changed. Though we were still nominally 'boyfriend and girlfriend', with the decision to finalise our son's adoption the dynamic had irrevocably shifted and not in a good way. I certainly no longer wanted to have sex with him. I was too scared, we both were. How could we even think about it after all the repercussions from before?

In truth, Tim and I were doomed from the moment I found out I was pregnant. As time passed I became full of resentment for how little the whole episode appeared to have impacted him. Though his parents had been angry, he hadn't been sent away. He'd escaped the stinging disapproval of strangers. He hadn't been humiliated or thrown into the great unknown of a mother and baby home. He hadn't felt the excruciating pain of labour or of being so alone in the hospital. He hadn't bathed and dressed and fed our child. He hadn't held our child close and felt the depth of that bond. Did he really understand what we'd lost or what it had been like for me? All these years later, as I write my book, I know that he has been deeply affected by everything, not quite in the same way as me but still with a great sense of sadness and loss for our son and the pain he could see in me.

Memory is such a funny thing. I know Tim was by my side when I went to the Magistrate's Court to sign the adoption papers, but I have no memory of us going there, being there, when it was, or signing any documents. I later learned it was June 1972 and that we had to pay £20 for the privilege. That doesn't sound like much but when you consider that the minimum weekly wage was £20 and the average weekly food bill for a British person at the time was £2.41, it starts to seem much more significant.

Particularly when you consider that Tim and I were both still at school.

Not long after that, Tim and I ended our relationship for good. We'd been staying at Emma's, who having left school had her own place in an area called Bear Flat. We went for a walk and talked it out. When the decision was made, we cried together. We were both sad as we cared deeply for each other but we both knew it was right. Perhaps we were both relieved in some way, thinking it would be easier to put the memory of Baby Tim behind us if we no longer had to look at each other. We could only begin again with people who didn't know our story.

Back in the classroom, I struggled to make up for the time I'd lost, but otherwise it was not as difficult to be back at school as I had expected it to be. Or maybe I just don't remember. I'm sure I would have assumed that my pregnancy must have been the talk of the convent but I don't recall it being that way at all. I certainly don't remember any of my former classmates asking me outright where I'd been for the past six months. Perhaps it would have been different if I were still in the fifth form. In the sixth form, we spent much less time together as a class. Many of my former classmates had left after O-levels and very few girls had chosen to study science A-levels, thus my circle had naturally grown smaller. There were far fewer opportunities for gossip. In any case, everyone was caught up in their own teenage dramas. My disappearance in the middle of the Christmas term was old news.

Emma had left the convent at the end of the fifth year so I started to spend more time at school with a girl called Maria who would become one of my closest friends – life-long. While I'd been at rock concerts with Tim, Dave and Emma, drinking cider and, eventually, getting myself into trouble, Maria belonged to a much less rebellious crowd. She would go to a place called the Four Square Coffee Bar, which was affiliated to her Catholic church. She met her husband Chris there.

Recently, I asked Maria whether she'd known that I was pregnant when I disappeared half-way through the first term of the lower sixth. She said that she'd had an inkling what might be going on, having seen me slumped over my desk in several exams, looking very tired and pale as I struggled to finish my papers. But she didn't know for sure until I told her the whole story, which she tells me was during that summer term. I swore her to secrecy and, to her enormous credit, she kept my secret for decades. She did not even tell her husband, who I am also great friends with now, until the day of my father's funeral, by which time circumstances were very different indeed. As a teenager, Maria was the perfect friend, keeping my secret when she might have bandied it about as gossip.

Chapter Seventeen

That year, I also became close to a girl called Bridget. On Wednesday afternoons, she and I, together with Maria, would go rowing on the river that ran through the city. It was offered as an alternative to doing PE in the school gym. Those afternoons on the river felt like rare carefree moments in my life, not least because we often took bottles of cider with us. I'm not sure I ever told Bridget what had happened to me.

Despite those cider-fuelled afternoons, I hadn't become a total rebel. I was also very active with social services, volunteering to work with a local disabled children's society. Bath Convent girls were expected to do work for the wider community but the zeal with which I approached my task spoke of a greater need to redeem myself.

Slowly, I began piecing my life back together as best I could. I'd had to give up my job at Woolworths when I went to St Anne's. Now I found a new one with clothing and interiors store Laura Ashley. Laura Ashley was not the big international business it is these days. Bath was the company's head office and the bosses, Jean and Peter Reevers, were very much hands-on. Though I was only a part time worker, on Saturdays and throughout every holiday, they treated me as a valued colleague, and it wasn't long before I was pretty much running the stockroom. I was even invited to spend a weekend at the Welsh country house that belonged to Laura Ashley herself.

Work gave me a degree of normality and a sense of achievement. It was harder to feel like I was achieving much at school. By the time I got back to the classroom in late April 1972 I'd missed an awful lot of lessons and had much to catch up on. I did not do well, failing my end of year exams apart from 50% in physics and in my chemistry practical and averaging 58% in statistics. I also had 'outstanding ability in dance and movement'. Regardless of my failures I was allowed to stay on at school for the Upper Sixth and to sit the real exams I was so badly prepared for.

My school report at the end of my first term in the Upper Sixth year makes interesting reading. When I went back to school, none of the teachers ever explicitly mentioned my having been pregnant. It's possible that some of them didn't even know that was why I'd been away. I received no extra support. Academically, I was expected to sink or swim. I hadn't caught up. That term, my A level mock exam marks ranged from 43% in Physics down to 5% in pure maths. In my report a couple of my teachers express surprise that I'm struggling, putting it down to insufficient revision. They abdicated responsibility. However, the new headmistress, Sister Angela, made a comment that suggested at least a little compassion and understanding. She wrote, 'Michelle must not be discouraged with these results. She was overtired when taking these exams and did not do herself justice.'

That was as good as it got. I was given no one-to-one support. I was just thrown back in and expected to carry on as normal. But life wasn't normal. Every day I wanted to scream, 'I want my baby, I miss him so much!'

Chapter Eighteen

Emma and I remained firm friends after she left school in the summer of 1971. She and Dave had split up about the same time as Tim and I parted and most of our evenings out were together. I used to stay over at Emma's flat, especially if we planned to be out late. My parents didn't object. I suppose the worst had already happened, as far as they were concerned. They also liked Emma which I'm sure must have helped.

Emma and I sometimes went to a little coffee house in Kingsmead Square. It had a jukebox on which I'd spend a small fortune playing the Chicken Shack version of the soulful Etta James song classic *I'd Rather Go Blind*. I played that song again and again and again. I'd stand by the jukebox and sing along, swaying to the music as it swept over me. The lyrics, about a woman knowing she's losing her man, oozed a sense of pain and a broken heart that seemed to echo my secret grief.

In September 1972, Tim went to university in Bristol. I saw him on two occasions after that, most memorably when Emma and I were in Bristol for some reason and we decided on a whim to stop by the flat-share where Tim was living with his student friends. We didn't even go inside. Instead, Tim leaned out of an upstairs window to speak to me. I'd come straight from school to join Emma. I've always wondered if Tim was embarrassed to see me there in my school uniform.

It was a weird and sad moment as I gained a sense that he had moved forward away from the pain and sorrow that was still weighing me down. As I looked up, I just saw a normal student enjoying his life. The boy who had been the centre of my world, with whom I had shared so much, whom loving had brought us both so much sadness, was no longer part of my life, despite us sharing a history that would be there, binding us together forever.

As well as spending time together in Bath , Emma and I also spent more time closer to my home and on the RAF Station where we'd lived when we first came to Bath. We started hanging out with a group of RAF guys who were interested in motorbikes. Moving forward was hard. But I needed a change of scene and to be away from reminders of my life with Tim, which could only add to the pain and sorrow of parting with my son. I think Emma also wanted to move on from her time with Dave. I was lucky that we remained firm friends.

Although I was not in a good place, I started dating again. After a false start with someone who really wasn't right for me, I met a guy called Tom and we soon started seeing each other.

I was 18. I was living at home with Mum and Dad, and Mum in particular was still trying hard to pretend that 1971 and 1972 had never happened. For that reason, I felt as though I could no longer be myself at home. I couldn't talk to Mum about anything. I felt abandoned and lonely. What's more, I felt like a terrible person. All I wanted was for my parents to view me as an 'acceptable' person again. I wanted to know I was still loved. I needed to be hugged and reassured. But despite my best efforts there was no sign of a thaw and home started to get so oppressive that I knew the only thing I could do was leave.

Chapter Eighteen

At the same time, my relationship with Tom had deepened into something more than a friendship. Tom was in love with me and I with him. We were serious about our relationship. He was being posted to Germany and he wanted me to go along. The only way that could happen was if he and I were to get married.

By this time, I had taken my A-levels and failed them all. My teachers and parents seemed surprised that I had not done better – though no-one had made any real effort to help me catch up the work I'd lost while I was banished to Chepstow. My university dreams were over. My academic failures increased the sense of disappointment my parents had in me. There was absolutely nothing keeping me in Bath. So when Tom asked me to be his wife, I told him I thought that would be a very good idea.

Tom was a well brought-up, thoughtful young man, so of course he decided he would have to formally ask my father for my hand. Dad respected the old-fashioned courtesy Tom showed on my behalf. After Tom's visit, Dad and I sat in the garden together and Dad asked me straight out.

'Does he know?'

He meant, of course, *does he know you've had a baby?*

'Yes Dad,' I said. 'Tom knows everything.'

'And he still wants to marry you?' was Dad's incredulous reply.

Thus, what should have been a moment of great happiness once again became an occasion for me to be reminded of my sin. I was tainted. I had given birth to a child out of wedlock. Dad believed this should truly stop someone from wanting to be with me. It says so much about how things were back then and how Dad's upbringing brought its own baggage.

Though Dad must have given Tom his blessing on that day, he and Mum spent the next few weeks doing their best to persuade me that getting married was a terrible idea. All their arguments went right by me. Though I felt bad about myself in so many ways, I was still pretty headstrong and I had decided that marrying Tom was the right thing for me. He was a decent man, he was kind, and I wanted to be with him.

So Tom and I got married in November 1973. It was a humorous occasion. Tom and I travelled to the register office together but on the way his car broke down. Luckily as a mechanic he was able to fix it, but it meant we were both late for our own wedding and Tom was covered in grease!

My parents were not at the ceremony to be by my side or to 'give me away'. But interestingly, Mum and Dad did put on a reception back at their house and worked hard to convince the guests that they were very happy to see their daughter wed. Perhaps they knew there was nothing they could do to change my mind and that all they could do was hope I'd made the right decision.

A couple of weeks later, Tom and I left for Germany. Here was a new beginning. I could leave my past behind. As we drove to Harwich and onwards from the Hook of Holland I was finally happy. I was with someone who loved me, someone who thought I was an ok person, not someone who had committed a terrible crime. We were setting off to start our new life together.

Chapter Nineteen

'Wherever you go, there you are.' Isn't that the saying? So much for me starting my new life. It turned out I brought my troubles with me. There was no way to outrun the deep sadness inside me.

Tom and I both went into our marriage in good faith but the truth was – as my parents must have known and tried to tell me – I was not at all ready for this new phase. At home in Bath, uncomfortable as it had been to live with my parents' disapproval pervading the atmosphere, I had been surrounded by the familiar and that made things easier to a degree. By contrast, Germany was entirely unfamiliar to me. I didn't speak the language. I didn't know the landscape. The strangeness of my new situation, not knowing anyone and without any friends reminded me of the moment I arrived at St Anne's, not knowing what awaited me inside. I was utterly thrown.

When we first arrived in Germany we were housed in a bedsit about 30 minutes away from the RAF Station. It was just one room with a bathroom across the hall. A little later we moved to a larger flat above a bar about the same distance away. I had no issue with the accommodation we were provided with because it turned out that wherever we lived was going to be a nightmare for me.

Tom had to work shifts. To begin with, being alone in the daytime was fine. I just became a wreck at night. I could not be left alone in the dark without feeling that something awful was going to befall me. I was this absolutely terrible person. I deserved for something bad to happen. It *was* going happen. It was just a question of time. Alone at night in the dark I became convinced that someone would break in and attack me and kill me for the terrible things I had done. I'd got pregnant outside marriage and given away my baby. I felt like a criminal. I had been treated like a criminal by my family and by society. I needed to be punished. I developed an unreasonable fear of death and an obsessive desire to check cupboards and other spaces for the presence of intruders. I was not well.

What a great start to a marriage! Poor old Tom. To be fair, I tried to keep how I was feeling from him so I'm not sure that hc was fully aware of the extent of the horror each night shift gave me. Every night I was alone I would hardly sleep. I would sit tense and frozen until Tom came home, then act as if all was well and that I'd had a good night while he was working. This act of being a chameleon is something that I have perfected over time and would come back to time and time again.

Hard as I tried to keep my anxiety under control, it wasn't long before I wouldn't, couldn't, go anywhere on my own. I was endlessly anxious, convinced that calamity was waiting just around the corner. It was unsafe outside and something dreadful would happen if I dared step out there.

Eventually I decided to seek help. The first GP I saw recognised and recorded that I had been badly affected by 'an illegitimate pregnancy' and 'since then things had gone from bad to worse'. The prognosis given was good, attributed to 'her good insight and intelligence' and because of the 'reactive nature of the situation'. It was decided that the best approach was to medicate me out of the situation and soon I was taking a rainbow of pills to calm my anxiety and fears and to help me sleep at night when on my own. The prescribing doctor also made reference to psychotherapy but as with so many other things I don't remember this. I'm going by what was written in my notes.

Although my 'illegitimate pregnancy' was recognised as the main contributing factor, I am not aware of any ensuing discussion on how being parted from my child was bound to affect how I was feeling and could lead to the symptoms I was experiencing. It is not *normal* to have a child, in my case a son, and then have to pretend he never existed. It seems incredible today that no-one joined the dots and explained to me why I was experiencing such fear of there being a big bad world around me, especially when I was anywhere that felt unfamiliar.

But that was the way it was. In those days you just didn't question a doctor's judgement. If they said I needed pills, then I'd take them. On my cocktail of powerful medications, I was pretty much out of it all of the time. I was sleep-walking through life. Poor Tom must have wondered what had happened to the woman he fell in love with. Scared and lonely and now medicated to the eyeballs, I was still falling apart.

Chapter Twenty

Luckily, after months of living in a drug-induced haze, I found my way to a GP who saw the long-term trouble I was storing up for myself by relying on such heavy medication to get me through the day. Rather than adding a set of new pills to my armoury, he sat me down and asked me what was going on. It was the first time in a very long time that someone had listened – really listened – to me. I poured my heart out, telling him everything that had happened to me.

Having considered what I told him, he said, 'Michelle, you need something to focus on.'

Something to focus on? What did that mean?

'You need a goal. You need a vision for your life.'

It sounded ridiculous. I was an RAF wife in a country that felt all too strange to me. I couldn't leave the house without knowing Tom was going to be there beside me. I didn't have the mental strength or energy to come up with a *vision*.

The doctor gently pressed me. I must have had goals once upon a time. What did I want to be when I was at school? he asked.

Why was that relevant? I was a shadow of the girl I'd once been and all the plans I'd had – to study at St Mary's and become a nuclear engineer – seemed like an impossible dream.

All the same, I shyly told the GP about my old university ambitions, which had fallen apart when I failed my A-levels.

'Why don't you re-take them?' the GP asked.

His question was so simple but so unexpected. Why didn't I retake my A-levels?

'Could I?'

'Of course you could.'

The kindly GP explained that on a nearby Army base was a school where I could enrol. It wouldn't cost me anything. I might be older than the average student but that didn't matter. What else was I going to do with my time while Tom was at work?

I left the GP's office that day feeling tentatively optimistic. It was as though I'd been standing in the middle of a dark forest, unable to see a way forward, until the GP handed me a torch with his careful questions. I could still only see a little way ahead, but that was all I needed to start to find a path out of the woods.

Just a few days later I enrolled at the base's secondary school and was immediately encouraged when I discovered that I wasn't going to be the oldest student in class after all. I quickly became friends with Davina, the daughter of an Army Major, about the same age as me. She was re-sitting her A-levels to improve her grades because she wanted to be a dentist. She didn't care if she had to sit in a room full of children to fulfil her ambitions. Years later, she too would become a Major.

Like Davina, once I overcame my self-consciousness about being back in the classroom, I took to studying like a duck to water. I dived into my books with an enthusiasm that had been distinctly lacking during my last few terms at the Convent. My 'all or nothing' nature came back into play and I was soon top of the class in maths, physics and chemistry. Forget Mogadon and Valium or something stronger. Studying became my new drug. It gave me a reason to get up in the morning. The 'vision for my life' the GP told me I needed began to take on clearer contours day by day. Perhaps my dreams were not impossible after all…

As my confidence started to grow and I slowly weaned myself off the various medications that had been keeping me in the fog – how I managed not to become addicted, I will never know – I was also able to go back to work. Tom had been supporting us both for so long and I was eager to start pulling my weight. I took whatever jobs I could find on the base. I worked in a fast-food restaurant, frying chips and burgers night after night. The heavy smell of chip fat would linger long after my shift finished, but I was happy to be bringing in some cash. I also started working as a lifeguard at the base's pool, echoing my first Saturday job back on the RAF station near Bath. There were often squaddies on leave from Northern Ireland at the pool. One of their favourite jokes was to pretend to get into difficulty so that I would dive to the rescue. It was good-hearted enough. They knew that if they gave me any real trouble, I would be straight on the phone to the military police.

There were a few things about being an airman's wife that made me laugh too, this occasion being one of them: I had toothache so I visited the dentist on the base. He injected me with anaesthetic to numb my gum while he drilled the offending tooth. The anaesthetic didn't take but when I complained that I was in pain while he removed the old filling, I got little sympathy.

Instead, Tom was hauled up in front of his commanding officer. He was told to keep his wife under control and to tell her – me – that I should not talk back.

'Tell her if the dentist says she's numb, she's numb,' the officer said, as if that would make a difference. There was definitely a 'status' thing going on!

My social life improved as well. I made friends with a couple of Tom's colleagues and their partners. Our German landlords were welcoming too, especially when we arrived with a three-litre bottle of duty-free Germany Asbach Brandy.

Tom and I also played bridge in a small group run by my Chemistry teacher. Tom was an experienced player and I was a novice. I hated it though, totally unable to grasp what it was about despite my mathematical mindset. At certain points Tom or my other partner players would say 'you know what to do now' and I wouldn't have a clue. However, it was a great way to ease myself back into making friends, in a quiet, companionable setting.

Day by day, every day, things got a little better. I'm sure that Tom was very happy to see me slowly coming back to life, but the problems for our marriage were really only just beginning.

Chapter Twenty-One

In the spring of 1975, just before I turned 20, I was dealt another blow. I had managed to pluck up the courage to take a trip back to the UK on my own. Though going back to school had given me confidence in many areas, travelling alone was still something I found hard. It was difficult to overcome my anxiety and get on board the flight from Germany to RAF Lyncham, but Tom saw me onto the plane and I reminded myself that my father would be meeting me at the other end. I would be on my own only for the length of the flight. Even then, I would be surrounded by other people from the base to whom I could turn in an emergency.

So I boarded the flight, carrying bags full of gifts for my parents and my little sisters, Christine and Anna. I was especially looking forward to seeing Anna. I was sure she would be delighted when she saw the German Easter treats I had packed for her.

Unfortunately, the flight did not go as smoothly as I had hoped. The plane was full of RAF regiment personnel on their way back from Northern Ireland for some well-deserved 'R&R' back in the UK; they were rowdy and noisy and when we landed at RAF Lyneham the military officers announced they were going to check the luggage of every single person on the flight. It took ages and I grew anxious again as I imagined my father waiting for me and wondering where I'd got to. I was also carrying far more duty free than the allowance and very little money.

Thankfully only the forces personnel were of interest. I was nodded through and I rushed to meet Dad. But he wasn't there. Instead, I was met by an RAF driver bearing a board with my name written on it.

I sensed at once that something was not right. My father was not senior enough to warrant a driver being sent to pick up his adult child. I got into the car and the driver took me to my parents' house. He didn't give me any clues as to why the pick-up plan had changed and of course I had no mobile phone and couldn't call ahead and solve the mystery that way. My sense of foreboding only grew stronger when we got to the little hamlet outside Bath. No-one was waiting at the window, looking out for my arrival as the driver pulled up. I prayed that nothing had happened to Mum or Dad.

As I no longer had a key to the house I had to knock on the door and wait to be let in. I shifted anxiously from foot to foot, with my bags full of gifts in my hands. Where was everybody?

When my mum and sister Christine came to door, they were both in floods of tears. They stood aside and I walked into the sitting room, still not knowing what to expect. There in the centre of the carpet, was a stand which supported a tiny coffin. Inside the open coffin was my dear little sister Anna.

Throughout her short life, my little sister Anna had often been unwell, frequently complaining of stomach aches. Born three months premature, she never quite seemed to thrive in the way that Christine and I both had. She always needed much more of our mother's care and attention.

On the day leading up to her death, Anna was in such pain that Mum and Dad had taken her to see their GP. The GP took one look at Anna and diagnosed a virus. His advice was that my parents should take their daughter home and put her to bed. The pain would pass, he assured them. But it didn't pass, and my parents had never seen Anna in such discomfort, so the next day, they tried again. This time they saw a doctor at the RAF base. He too told my parents to take Anna home. He said she would be fine with a good night's rest, despite, according to my parents, her writhing in agony in front of him. Back at home Anna was not fine. But my parents had the words of two doctors ringing in their ears now and it was a Bank Holiday. They didn't dare disturb another doctor for a third opinion. Anna died that night.

A post mortem to discover the cause of Anna's death revealed that she had a tissue obstruction in her intestine. My understanding is it had likely been there since she was born, perhaps explaining her life-long poor health. In the days leading up to her death, that piece of tissue must have somehow closed off Anna's intestine altogether. It's impossible to be sure but had she been seen by a specialist, perhaps things might have turned out differently and Anna might have lived.

It was the most awful homecoming but it was also a watershed moment. My parents were devastated. From Anna's death on, Mum treated me differently. Though she would not discuss it explicitly, she began trying to make up for the anger and pain that had come between us. This confirmed in my mind when she said to me 'I now know what it is like to lose a child'.

After this, it was as if she could not do enough to take care of me whenever I came home, especially by taking the time to cook interesting and wholesome meals for me. But we never discussed how she felt to lose Anna or how I felt to lose Baby Tim. It is really so sad because I am sure that if either one of us had the courage to open up the conversation, we could have both done so much healing.

I found out when I got back to Germany that Tom had known about my sister's sudden death before I left for my trip to England. My father had called him with the bad news, but swore him to secrecy. I was already due to come home in a matter of days and Dad thought that hearing about Anna's death would be too upsetting for me to deal with while travelling. Tom agreed. He and Dad both believed that they were protecting me by keeping me in the dark, as if I were a small child.

Like Baby Tim, my sister Anna soon became a subject we just didn't talk about at all. My father's time in Siberia, his time floating in the Atlantic and his service experiences in WW2 and afterwards gave him great resolve to survive whatever came his way. My mother too with her experiences of Russian occupation and surviving wartime in Germany was used to soldiering on. Genetically and experientially, for us Pearsons it was a matter of fact that hardships can be endured; they can be overcome.

Mum and Dad would never have considered counselling to help them deal with the emotional fall-out of their youngest daughter's death. They would have thought that was self-indulgent, perhaps even pointless after the fact. Talking wouldn't bring Anna back. Just as talking wouldn't bring Baby Tim back to me. Though in the years to come, I would try all sorts of counselling to endeavour to put my own life back together, I would never have told Mum and Dad about it or suggest they tried the same. It simply wasn't their way.

They wanted to find a way to move on and their strategy to achieve this was to bury the tragedy deep within and carry on. I tried to follow their example.

Chapter Twenty-Two

Back in Germany, I passed my A-levels, getting A grades in physics and maths and a C grade in chemistry, which was lower than everyone expected but still good enough to earn me a place on a university course. Suddenly I was ambitious about university again.

Looking back, I can see that continuing with my education wasn't just for my own satisfaction. My parents had been very pleased to hear that I was going to re-sit my A-levels and they were delighted with my results. To have them actually approve of something I'd done again, after such a long period of feeling like a huge disappointment to them, made me feel as though perhaps they were beginning to thaw in their attitude towards me. Doing well in my studies was a way back into their good books. It was the path to forgiveness. Their praise and acknowledgement was like a drug to me. I longed to be loved again, to be forgiven, to be accepted back into the family as a 'good girl', and a worthy daughter. Soon I needed bigger and bigger hits.

This was when a new era in my life was born – that of driving myself ever harder. The only thing that mattered to me was regaining acceptance with anyone and everyone, whatever the personal price. It was not exactly a sustainable and healthy approach but one that I would manage to live by and maintain for many years to come. It was also a way to manage secrecy and shame. If I was always too busy to think about it, I could keep the pain and sadness out of my conscious thoughts and get through – one day at a time.

In the summer of 1976, the whole of Europe was baking in one of the worst heatwaves for years. Having finished my A levels, I remember chilling out on the sunny afternoons lying in a hammock. Life was easier. Meanwhile, Tom and I had been married for almost two years and naturally, he wanted to make plans for the future. Coming from a family of four children and being a great older brother, Tom wanted to have a family, but how could I even consider it? The very thought filled me with sadness and guilt. I had already had a child and I'd given him up. How on earth could I risk having another? Getting pregnant again was not what I wanted. It was clear I was 'unfit' to be a mother – after all, I had been told that by the very act of adoption. I was far too scared and felt unable to cope emotionally.

I didn't say any of this to Tom. Not only did I skirt around the issues, I dropped the bombshell that I wanted to go to university. I could tell at once that Tom wasn't keen on the idea – it meant at least another three years when I wouldn't want to think about starting a family – but he was good enough to try to come to a compromise.

Tom already knew that his time in Germany was due to end and he would be sent back to the UK. He agreed that he would only apply for postings to RAF stations close to university towns. We narrowed that down to two, one in Essex and one in North Wales. Essex was my first choice – to study Chemical Physics – purely because that's where Tom expected to go. I got a place there, but I kept a place for the same subject at Bangor University as back-up and, in the end, that was where I would go, while Tom worked at RAF Valley on the Welsh island of Anglesey.

For the time being at least, I had succeeded in finding a way to continue my path to redemption with my parents as well as postpone facing the truth about how the loss of Baby Tim was still affecting me in ways that I couldn't even begin to articulate.

Chapter Twenty-Three

Tom and I moved back to the UK in the late summer of 1976. We had nowhere to live but I had been in contact with my future tutor Pat, who kindly invited us to stay with his family until we found a place of our own. Pat and his wife Anne were a delightful couple. Anne, a local GP before having a family, was well known for walking her goats on leads around the neighbourhood like other people would walk their dogs.

Eventually and in time for the start of term Tom and I were allocated married quarters at RAF Valley. Bangor University was 20 miles away from our house and I didn't have a car or even know how to drive. Neither was there a suitable bus that would get me to my morning classes on time. My only option was to get up before dawn and set off at five am to walk to a lay-by on the A5 where I waited for a man who worked as a chef in the university halls to give me a lift.

It wasn't much fun to do that walk in all weathers, but I was glad to do it because it was the only way I could fulfil my dream of getting a degree. I was so excited to be sitting in a lecture hall, just as my 15-year-old self had once planned, I would have walked twice as far for the privilege. I was a dedicated student, making sure my work was the best it could be. While many of my fellow students were more interested in the freedom of being away from home for the first time, for me the student bar was of little interest. I was making up for lost time and I had something to prove. I knew that Dad was very pleased I had a place at university. With my drug-like addiction for acceptance and redemption, all I needed to do now was make sure I came away with a first-class degree.

The unspoken bar I felt I needed to jump for my parents' approval was getting higher and higher. Added to that, I needed to keep my mind so full of maths and physics that there wasn't room for the sadness of losing my son to creep back in. I could not risk having time to dwell on the past. My new drive to become a world class scientist kept thoughts of Baby Tim at bay.

It was hard work, juggling university life with being an RAF wife. At the end of a long day of studying, I would catch a train back towards the RAF Station. Sometimes Tom would pick me up from the University, but increasingly often he wouldn't. The tensions at home were growing.

'Do you have to study again, Michelle?'

'Are you suggesting we go out somewhere?' I was always keen to go walking or out for a meal.

'How about we just curl up on the sofa together and watch TV? There's a really good programme on later.'

'Tom, if all we're going to do is watch TV, I'm going to study.'

I never saw the point of watching TV when I had much more interesting things to do, like study quantum physics! I don't think I was ever destined to be a proper wife, at least the one he had imagined he was marrying. I was moving away from Tom emotionally and through my new interests. The writing was on the wall.

This was very unfair on Tom as he was a decent man and all he wanted was a good family life. I was just psychologically unable to give him what he needed. We were worlds apart.

Soon, our relationship became unsustainable and, gathering my courage, just before the end of my first year at Bangor I asked Tom for a divorce. He was not at all happy about it and did his best to persuade me against it. He tried to convince me that he was pleased for me to be at university and we could still make it work. Sticking to my guns, I told him that I was leaving.

I moved out into a small female only student hall. It was a refuge for me. Then in the summer holidays, I thought that I would give our marriage another go thinking that maybe the exams had been stressing me out. But it wasn't just the exams. In the October, I moved out again. I remember leaving carrying all my possessions in a single suitcase. It was not anyone's fault, just the result of a mismatch of time and circumstances. Tom was a delightful man who deserved so much better than I was able to give him. I married him in good faith but I sometimes wonder if we would have married so soon, or at all, had he not been posted to Germany so early on in our relationship.

I had begun my first year at university as Tom's wife, living in married quarters on the RAF Station. I began my second year as a normal single student, moving into shared accommodation in Bangor where everything was in walking distance. I was very glad to be able to say 'goodbye' to the five o'clock in the morning starts.

The house I moved into should have been condemned. Instead, it was home to almost a dozen people. I shared a flat on the top floor with Ellie, a first-year female physics student. Females were few and far between in our department, so it was natural for us to seek each other out. On the floor beneath us, lived a family with several children, and below them another group of single students. We had just one bathroom between all of us.

The house was in a terrible state. It had no central heating and was cold and damp no matter the weather outside. The bathroom was always filthy, as you can probably imagine given that it was being shared by so many people. Mice roamed wherever they pleased. I would often wake up in the night to find a particularly daring rodent scampering right across my bed covers, if not my face (I was sleeping on a mattress on the floor). They weren't in the least bit afraid of human beings. Most days Ellie and I would sit in our little kitchen, with our feet up from the floor, and watch the rubbish bag move or the mice run around our kettle.

The family below us kept very different hours to me and Ellie, which was good given the bathroom situation as it meant we all had a better chance of being able to get in there, but difficult when they turned the music up just as we wanted to go to sleep. Coming from Jamaica they loved reggae and through the nights I became very familiar with *Do the Reggae* by Toots and the Maytals and artists such as Bob Marley. They were very friendly and often invited us to join them for the evening and share their food, usually dried cod (saltfish) and extremely hot chilli sauce.

The house might have been squalid and noisy, but my memories of my time there are ultimately very happy. I'd gone from living with my parents straight to living with a husband. Now I had a degree of real freedom for the first time in my life.

I look back on this as one of the best years of my life. I was enjoying my studies, I was making friends, and I felt good about myself and relatively carefree.

Although my fears had evaporated in that I didn't go round thinking that danger was lurking everywhere, I still had a lot of problems to deal with on a daily basis. I suffered from terrible panic attacks, as I had in Germany. They would happen without warning, more often than not while I was in a lecture theatre. I was getting better at managing them as the year before they had been even worse but they were still paralysing. I remember vividly the first one at Bangor. I was still a new student, everything was unfamiliar. I was in a lecture theatre with around 100 other students, all male and mostly electronic engineers who shared a few physics lectures with my cohort. Suddenly I was unable to breathe and this great wave of fear, over nothing specific, overwhelmed me. I was terrified that I was about to pass out, or worse still that I was about to die.

'Are you ok?' asked the young man sitting next to me.

But I was unable to answer. My heart was pounding in my chest and a sense of numbness had built up in my arms and legs and now extended into my chest, making it hard to breathe, never mind speaking. I could see the look of concern, then puzzlement in his face.

Finally, I managed to say 'I'm fine'.

I quickly turned my head away. I did not want any attention on me. I rested my head on my hand with it covering that side of my face putting a barrier between us. I looked down at my notes, desperately trying to focus on something that would help the attack subside. The all too familiar sense that something dreadful was about to happen to me and that I had no control over what that would be was becoming unbearable. It was surreal, like I was not there in the here and now. I could barely hear what was being said in the lecture and my awareness of the young man next to me and the others in the hall felt totally distorted. From my previous experiences I knew the attack would pass but in that moment any clarity of thought was elusive. Thankfully the lecture hall was relatively dark and my fellow student went back to concentrating on what was being said by the lecturer. Eventually I could feel the attack subside and normality descend upon me, my shoulders and whole body relaxing. Now I was just exhausted. As soon as the lecture was over and the lights went up, I bolted out of the hall. I was too embarrassed to stay and risk being asked again if I was ok.

From that day on, to reduce drawing any attention to myself, and because I couldn't bear feeling physically hemmed in by people, I always spread my books out to create physical space around me. I also made sure I sat at the back and at the end of a row in the lecture theatres. Even when I couldn't move I had to know I had an escape route. Something I still need to do to this day in cinemas, theatres or any situation where I have people around me. I always need to know I can leave unhindered.

At times I'm not sure how I managed to keep up with my studies, but thankfully I did. Away from lectures, I did my best to mitigate any residual feelings of anxiety with busyness.

Term time was full of study and the holidays full of work. I worked as a cleaner, a shop assistant and latterly as a Saga Tour guide in Bangor. I needed the money to live but as with anything else, I approached every job with enthusiasm and gave of my best.

I also loved studying, especially theoretical physics and organic chemistry: a rather odd combination but one I was able to follow throughout my time as an undergraduate via the modules that were available within my degree choice of Chemical Physics. The course had not been designed to enable students to follow this combination of interests, but it did not preclude it. It was odd really as I ended up doing more theoretical physics modules than many of the physicists and more of the organic chemistry modules than most of the chemists.

As you might expect, I continued to set myself high achievement targets. My first mark for a piece of coursework was in the mid-seventies and it was the lowest mark threshold that I would allow for myself. So straight away I drove myself to do well. There was only one other student doing chemical physics alongside me – an extremely bright, likeable and very young Welshman, Dafydd. And I am pleased to say we are still great friends today. Setting myself the competitive goal of doing better than him also came into play. I was so delighted in year two when I achieved this by a fraction of one percent! How silly really. By then nothing less than a first-class honours degree would be an acceptable level of achievement. I needed to be redeemed and to be seen by my parents as a 'good girl'. I wanted to be the daughter who would make them and their forebears proud. I wanted to fulfil their aspirations from when I was first born, knowing how important these were to them, given their own family histories.

Chapter Twenty-Four

While on the outside, I may have seemed like any other young student, enjoying my carefree life, things were always simmering away inside. I was doing a good job of keeping my Baby Tim in the back of my mind, by focussing so hard on my studies, but in January and February things would bubble up to the surface.

Apart from my son's birthday, which was always hard, there were other days when I felt especially and inexplicably sad. I would be filled with a grief to which I could not give a voice. Years later, when I read my adoption agency file and learnt about all the important dates – Tim's christening, the day we parted, key meetings with the social worker and the day the final decision was made – I realised that the body never forgets.

Back then I did not know where in the country my Baby Tim was living or even if he was still alive. Was he in the UK or in some other part of the world? I had no idea. But from time to time, I would see a child about his age with the sort of thick dark hair I knew he must have and my heart would leap. Was that him? How would I know? The thought that I might not recognise him broke my heart.

Was he healthy and happy? He must have started school. I wondered whether he was enjoying it, as I had when I was his age. Was he the sort of eager schoolchild I had once been myself? Was he finding it easy to learn how to read or do maths?

I imagined him sitting on his adoptive mother's knee as she helped him turn the squiggles on the pages of his reading book into words. I know I would have been a good teacher for him, were he still with me.

When I gave Baby Tim up, adoption was a far more closed process than it is now. The idea was that adoption entirely severed the baby's relationship with their birth family. His original birth records – his birth certificate and the correspondence between me and the adoption agency – would be sealed, never to be seen again. I was not told Baby Tim's new name, so that I would not be tempted to track him down. Had his adoptive parents told him about me? Had they even told him that he was adopted?

All these questions haunted me. I pushed them down as hard as I could into the back of my mind, telling myself that there was no point thinking about something I couldn't change. I also had to keep the secret of ever having had a child, at least from all except my closest friends. I had to stick to the Pearson family way of dealing with grief. Keep moving forward. Keep busy. Pretend it never happened.

Chapter Twenty-Five

By the start of the third year I was genuinely enjoying the freedom of being my own person. Yes, I had a few things to cope with, like the panic attacks, but even these had reduced in frequency and intensity. Overall life was just so wonderful compared with all the tough stuff I had dealt with before. But the delicate carapace I had built for myself was about to be shattered and my fragile new identity was about be tested again.

Term started for me at a party, when my eyes met – across a crowded room, as the cliché goes – with those of a young man. The attraction for both of us was instant and total and I knew we were destined to be together. Imagine my delight when I discovered he lived two doors down from me in the Halls I had just moved into. His name was Ian.

Ian and I started seeing each other and the attraction we'd felt on first meeting only deepened. He was in his first year and so much younger than me, especially since I had started three years later than most, but it was love. We had fun, we laughed and we shared good times. I felt relaxed and comfortable and free to be with him. When we were alone in my room or his, he would play his guitar for me. Sometimes he would play the famous guitar solo from *Stairway To Heaven*. As well as evoking all sorts of poignant memories of 1971, it became the piece of music I most associated with Ian. To this day it still reminds me fondly of him and the happiness he brought into my life.

It was clear that Ian adored me and I felt the same way about him. The first two terms of that academic year were such happy times for me. Ian had an old Triumph Bonneville and we would ride off up into Snowdonia or walk on beautiful and romantic beaches, such as Newborough on Anglesey, made all the more glorious with the glow of a magical sunset. Life was great. At the end of the Easter term, Ian took me home to meet his parents. I remember walking through some amazing bluebell woods near their home and feeling such peace and joy. But there was something about being with someone who seemed to like me so much that set me on an emotional rollercoaster again.

The problem was… me. I was unlovable in my own eyes and had no confidence in myself within the relationship. The big issue that I brought was my own uncertainty about myself and my ability to be Ian's partner. The feeling of worthlessness I'd had since saying goodbye to Baby Tim made me seek constant reassurance yet I couldn't accept it when it was given.

It wasn't long before I got it into my head that Ian was bound to dump me at some point. This relationship was so good it could not last – something was going to happen and it would be taken away from me. I did not deserve such happiness. This got progressively worse throughout the third term and near my final exams, I was all over the place. I was convinced that Ian would realise what a worthless person I was and that would be the end of it. He had done nothing to indicate this was about to happen. It was me in catastrophe mode. My own thoughts were terrifying.

* * *

This sudden tsunami of inner turmoil nearly cost me my degree. My focus was utterly shattered. Having done so well in my first two years at Bangor, I was at risk of missing my sacred goal of achieving a first. It took everything I had to get through my final exams. Somehow I managed to hold it together enough and the love of my subject saw me through but, physically and mentally, it was a tough time. Something inside me was determined to self-sabotage. I was not allowed to be as happy as Ian made me. He must have been baffled by the way I'd begun to behave when everything had been so good.

Having achieved a first-class honours degree in Chemical Physics, I knew I could stay in Bangor to do a PhD and that was what I wanted to do. But my fears about my relationship with Ian meant that I was worried about staying. I could see another girl circling round him. She had made it clear to me that she had plans for them to be together. Ian was oblivious to this, but it rocked my confidence further. What if he became attracted to her?

If Ian broke our relationship off, I would be stuck in the same town, constantly in danger of bumping into him, maybe even with this other girl. I knew I could not cope with that. If he broke up with me, it would be someone telling me, once again, that I was indeed unlovable. To avoid all of this, I needed to stay in control. I needed to be the one to finish the relationship. I felt I would cope so much better that way. So, sadly, that is just what I did. Instead of staying on for a PhD and enjoying what I had that was so good, I decided to go to London to do a Masters at Imperial College.

'I thought you wanted to do a PhD?' I could see the confusion and sadness in Ian's eyes as I told him my decision.

On the day I left Bangor, Ian insisted on taking me to the train.

'Why do you have to go, Michelle?' he asked me one more time.

'I have to do this, Ian. I'm so sorry.'

I climbed on to the train. As it pulled away, with tears streaming down my face I watched Ian stand on the platform with his hands upwards and a slight shoulder shrug to emphasise his 'why?'

Years later, I saw Ian again, quite by chance, at a sailing club where I was with Stephen (now my husband). I was happy and settled but, I have to say, my heart still skipped a beat when I saw him, the man who I had loved so much. Very sadly a year or so later, Ian was killed when his motorbike collided with a van near the sailing club. That must have been a terrible experience for his girlfriend at the time, who was following in her car.

The odd thing is that I did not know that Ian had had an accident and had been killed, but I suddenly started dreaming and thinking about him. Later on, I discovered that my thoughts and dreams about him were around the time of his death – how weird is that? I was very upset, as he was, and still is, very special to me. I would have loved to have taken part in a celebration of Ian's life with all his family and friends but sadly I was unaware of what had happened at the time. I still feel that I lack closure and have not fully grieved for him. I still think of him with a lot of fondness and keep a picture of us above my desk.

Chapter Twenty-Six

1980

The Masters Programme at Imperial College Business School was modular in nature and I specialised in Finance and Operational Research. It was the very early days of computer modelling of financial markets and took me in a totally new direction, ultimately leading me to a firm of stockbrokers and later to a merchant bank. I loved it. I loved being at the leading edge of my field forging into uncharted territory. It was exciting and 180 degrees away from how I felt about venturing into unfamiliar places in my day-to-day life.

It's hard to believe that colour computer screens had only just come onto the market. As a pioneering business user, I was invited to speak at several European business conferences. This led me to join the sponsoring company, a big American IT giant; a household name. My timing and skill set were perfect and after an intensive 18 months of training I became the client manager, looking after the London Stock Exchange, just as the City was about to go through a period of immense change, known as Big Bang.

I was one of very few women in this line of work. In my first post training role, I was the account manager for a very traditional insurance company and when I was leaving them to work full time with the Stock Exchange, my main contact called me in to say goodbye and he asked 'Will we be getting a man next time?'

At the Stock Exchange things were very different but there was still at least one floor in the building without a ladies' cloakroom and whenever I was there for lunch, I always had to go down a flight of stairs.

I was never going to be a traditional sales person. For me it was always about venturing outside areas where we were already established. At the Stock Exchange this took me to a small but visionary team, working on the potential for emerging technologies. This meant going to the States.

I always agreed to go of course, although the thought of having to travel by myself immediately filled me with anxiety. At this point I could keep most aspects of my life on an even keel, yet I had not managed to overcome my fear of travelling, especially to new places alone. Every time I had to go somewhere new, I became my 16-year-old-self arriving at St Anne's again. But what could I do? If nothing else I am always the professional, I always do my job and I do it well. I kept quiet and steeled myself for the challenges ahead.

I made several trips to the East Coast and often had the added challenge of travelling back and forth between Washington and New York. On two occasions in the States when I was back in my hotel room, I found myself struggling for breath, clutching at my chest as the pain went right through me like a kitchen knife slicing through my ribs. Each time I ended up in the emergency department of the local hospital, convinced as I lay on a trolley beneath the bright lights with chaos all around me that this was it. I was going to die right there, thousands of miles away from home. I was sure I must be having a heart attack. To my mind there was no other rational explanation.

Obviously, I did not die. The emergency doctors ran a number of tests and on both occasions assured me that there was absolutely nothing wrong with my heart. The second time, the doctor in charge of my care took me to one side and told me that my symptoms were due to overwork and the level of stress I was putting myself under, especially with my high travel-related anxiety. He advised me to take some time off and relax. I had to take better care of myself.

This was the eighties. It would be decades before it became acceptable to talk about mental health issues in the workplace. I was convinced that any admission of suffering from stress or anxiety would only have received a response along the lines of, 'Then perhaps this isn't the job for you. There's the door'.

No-one I worked with would have believed how bad things were at times. I was resourceful and developed some amazing strategies to hide my anxiety. On another flight to the US, a flight attendant noticed I seemed nervous.

'Are you OK?' she asked.

'I'm a nervous passenger,' I replied with some caution, not wanting to share exactly how uncomfortable I was.

She stayed to chat with me for a while.

'We help children to get through their anxieties about flying by having them help serve the meals,' she said.

'I wish I could do that,' I replied.

'Well…' The attendant looked to her supervisor. 'I don't see why you shouldn't.'

So I joined the flight attendant as she pushed her trolley up and down the cabin, dishing out trays of food and serving drinks. I started to enjoy myself. It was fun. All was going well until I turned to the next row of passengers and came face to face with a senior manager from my client, who I was due to meet with in New York.

'Michelle?' he said with a quizzical look on his face. 'What are you doing handing out meals?'

Quick as a flash, I responded. 'Company cost-cutting exercise.'

I was always quick with a joke to cover what was really happening for me. The incident wasn't mentioned at our meeting but I suspect, if asked, that senior manager would still be bemused today.

When I started work at the stockbrokers, I moved into a top floor flat – essentially three bed-sitting rooms with a shared kitchen and bathroom – part of an artist's house in South Hampstead, a lovely residential area close to Swiss Cottage and Finchley Road tube stations. I lived there for a few years, until I was settled at the IT company. Over this time my flatmates were an eclectic bunch – including a fellow Imperial College graduate, a Belgian doctor with years of experience working for MSF, an American Psychologist, a trainee-chartered accountant, a Foreign Office Management Trainee and a work colleague, Liz.

Cocktail bars were all the rage in the eighties and, as well as frequenting famous places like Rumours on the edge of Covent Garden, we were lucky enough to have a good one next to Finchley Road station where we could all meet up on our way home from our respective workplaces.

Most nights we would take it in turns to cook and our individu-al groups of friends became part of a wider circle we shared. Work was also a very social environment, especially at the stockbrokers. The few females outside the administrative roles were regularly invited out by the partners to nightclubs such as Annabel's. It was such fun. The partners were chivalrous and looked after us well. They always made sure we were taken home by black cab. Though on some nights, we got home so late there was little time before we needed to be ready to set off back to work.

It many ways I found it hilarious. I never really looked the part compared to others in their designer clothes and makeup, with their fashionable hairstyles. I remember my work colleague, friend and flatmate Liz, trying so hard to update me – arranging for me to have a cut and perm, the trend at the time. She herself was a Farrah Fawcett-Majors lookalike, immaculate and glamorous at all times. At one point she was dating a colleague from the city. She proudly showed me her latest birthday present, a Cartier watch. Sadly it did not have the effect she was seeking as I'd never heard of the brand, other than knowing there were cigarettes sold under that name! I think I was a lost cause.

At one level I was very settled and I felt the most carefree I had ever been. The secrecy surrounding Baby Tim was less of an issue as thankfully none of my friends had started thinking about having children, despite being of an age where it was common to do so. However, there was still so much pain etched on my heart and my inner struggles to deal with it continued.

My very good university friend Pat remembers coming to visit me in my flat-share a number of times. I thought I'd been hiding my feelings well, but she saw how troubled I was. In her words 'you talked about how you had been harmed' and 'it was obviously on your mind a lot'. I was clearly still trying to process what had happened to me, trying to make sense of its ongoing impact and how I could survive it.

No-one I lived or worked with would have believed how bad things were at times. Even Pat, living in another city, was not fully aware. Looking back now, it seems obvious why my sadness would increase around the important anniversaries of my time with my Baby Tim. Things would still sneak up on me, often without conscious realisation. Every November and December I'm sure part of me was, albeit unconsciously, reliving my total sense of rejection upon my banishment to the mother and baby home.

January brought with it the anniversary of Baby Tim's birth and that milestone continued to be particularly painful. As January 13th approached each year I would wonder where my baby, then my young boy, and now my teenager Tim, was and what he was doing. I had so many questions. Was he going to have a birthday party? Was he happy? Did he know he was adopted? Did he remember me? And the worst worry just as always – was he still alive?

The sadness I felt was of so much loss. I'm sure my anxiety was bound up with having felt so abandoned as a 16-year-old; of having been thrust into so many unknowns and with being unable to share my grief. I would often sit in my room in the flat or take myself off somewhere else that was private and cry my eyes out.

By 1987, things were beginning to change. Property, although expensive, was significantly cheaper South of the River Thames and just about everyone I liked spending time with had moved to Clapham and Wandsworth. By now I was well established at the IT company with plans to build my career there, so I did the same. I loved my one bedroom first floor flat and the location. I was within walking distance to the majority of my friends and we would regularly meet up for summer picnics on the common or at local restaurants and wine-bars. But things were also shifting for many of my friends.

As we were getting older deeper relationships were forming, people were getting married and children were starting to arrive.

Not for me though, as since I had been in London, no-one seemed to want to go out with me in a romantic way – at least no-one I fancied. It is true to say that there were men who were interested in me and I became great friends with two or three, but anyone I felt a spark for seemed to run a mile. I used to walk around Hyde Park and then Clapham Common wondering 'what is wrong with me? Why doesn't anyone want me?' At a deeper level, I 'knew' it was because I was unlovable. I was so full of shame and guilt for my past actions. Given that I was living this strange double life, outwardly chirpy but managing a myriad of complex emotions and challenges on the inside, it's perhaps no surprise that I spent the best part of 10 years single.

Thankfully I had a couple of solid male friends. Peter, who left Bangor for London a year before me, had taken me under his wing. Like a big brother he was always there for me, even when in a relationship of his own. I became part of his circle of friends and spending time with them was a haven for me as it was always social, never deep, and somewhere I could escape to.

While living near Finchley Road, I had also become good friends with an interior designer. He had a great interest in theatre, being somewhat theatrical himself. Over the years I knew him he had completed commissions for several well-known actors and I was often his partner at famous West End shows, and as a guest at several after-parties. He loved socialising and was always a willing partner for my work-related events.

Jack was a lovely man and like me was single. His search for a life partner (this being in the days before civil partnerships or same sex marriages were allowed) was proving difficult and I think it suited both of us to be able to go out to together, knowing that there was no possibility of us developing a romantic relationship. Mind you, there were a few complicated moments. He wanted to be a father and he saw me as the perfect person to mother his child; announcing it one day to a roomful of guests at his flat.

He had first raised the possibility of co-parenting at the Churchill Hotel in London, where he and I were staying, in adjoining rooms, as part of one of my work events. Having a child with Jack was never going to be the right thing for me to do, but I shared the story with my mum and between us it was affectionately known as the 'Winston Plan', in a nod to the name of hotel where the plan was proposed (which was of course named for Winston Churchill). It was actually lovely that despite all the history, my mum and I had made peace. Although we never talked about my son or the adoption, I could talk with her about anything else.

I think the time that my single status bothered me the most was the year I was rewarded for my sales achievements with an invitation to 'The Golden Circle'. This was an event to recognise 'exceptional achievers' and recipients of the award would enjoy a week away at a spectacular location with their spouses, which in the vast majority of cases, meant wives.

This particular year it was at Paradise Island in the Bahamas. Jack was delighted when I asked him to accompany me. I was so excited – a week in the sun with one of my best friends. He would be the perfect partner for the week, I knew how much fun he was to socialise with; always pleased for me and proud of me when he came to any business event. I don't know how but he even knew someone at the elite Ocean Club Hotel on the Island and promised to take me out for a meal there. I was so looking forward to the trip, despite the flying! The whole thing would be such a great reward for all my hard work.

Imagine my disappointment when my manager informed me that because I was single, I was not allowed to take a partner with me. I had to go on my own. I cannot begin to convey fully what hell it was to travel there and to spend a week in a magnificent setting, surrounded by couples who were being pampered. Rather than large corporate style dinners, couples would be booked into restaurants around the island for intimate romantic dinners. I was expected to endure going out for dinner at my assigned restaurants, not on my own, but paired up with a different single man every night. I gave this a go for the first two evenings, but sitting in such romantic settings with strangers, who probably felt as uncomfortable as I did, was dreadful. There were even specially themed items on the table to remind you of the importance of your partner and to thank them for their support. It was such a relief to be back on my own in my own room.

Even during the day, us singles were expected to 'team up' for any of the scheduled activities. It felt like punishment rather than a reward! I was furious when I discovered that another single person had actually smuggled their partner in and were just doing their own thing. Furious at myself; that I had been too compliant to think of this and now it was too late.

It got to the point where I really couldn't stand being in the midst of all the couples having such a lovely time. I had to do something to shift my perspective and find a way to make the most of this all-expenses-paid luxury trip away. I kept telling myself to find some gratitude and that I was very fortunate to have this experience, one that I could only dream of had it not been via work. I discovered the Club Med resort on the Island. I found a way to sneak in and I spent the rest of the week on the club beach by myself with a good book. I made sure I was back in my hotel for the buffet lunches that were set out in several places. I would plate something up and store this back in my room ready for my lone dinner. By the end of the week I actually felt restored and had enjoyed myself, despite a heightened awareness of the loneliness of not having someone special in my life, romantically.

It also reminded me of the isolation that can come from being single, even within a group of people you know. Some time earlier I had helped to 'matchmake' a colleague at work with one of my flatmates. Eventually they ended up getting married. Once settled in their new home, south of the river, they invited me to a house-warming dinner party. Before the evening arrived, the husband took me to one side.

'Please make sure you bring a man with you, the evening is a couples thing,' he said.

This was appalling on so many fronts. Not only had I been an unmarried mother and someone who gave their baby away. Now I was also a single person and heaven forbid, you have one of those in your house! To this day I wonder what would have happened if I had turned up with a woman partner. Needless to say, I didn't go to the 'couples dinner party' and I'm not sure I saw much of either of them again.

Chapter Twenty-Seven

Work had become my anchor. Doing well was so important to me. It gave me a reason to exist. I had failed as a mother. I was unfit to be one. At work I was successful. I had an identity. I was particularly proud of what I had achieved with my current client, still the London Stock Exchange. I had developed the strategic relationship to the point where a joint venture was under discussion and I wanted to stay working with them to see this through to a successful outcome.

My company had other ideas. I felt like the rug was being pulled from under my feet when I was asked, or rather told, to take over the management of a client where we had lost a lot of business over the previous years. My role was to rebuild the relationship. No matter how much I listened to the good it would do for my career, it was not what I wanted. Someone else was going to reap the rewards of all my hard work with the London Stock Exchange (LSE). I felt I had no choice and I made the move reluctantly.

Doing well at work also meant I was firmly on that righteous path to redemption with my parents. Whenever I felt this was at risk, I found it hard to cope. This was also put to the test when

I became close friends, or so I thought, with someone at work. I shared my adoption story with them only to find they broke my trust. I became office gossip. I felt so vulnerable emotionally, with my fear of being judged and my career cast adrift.

These two things happening at around the same time were very unsettling for me. I had put so much of myself into working with the LSE and my trust in my friend had been broken. My reaction to the second was easy to understand but my reaction to the first seemed too strong. I liked new challenges, so what was going on? My medical notes show that I recognised that I needed help and that I started to see a counsellor attached to St George's Hospital around this time. His comments reveal so much:

'The work episode… in which she pioneered, one might say, gave birth to, an important project only to have it taken away from her and the rewards given to someone else, so clearly parallels what happened to her with Tim 16 years earlier. Another baby being born but then taken when she gave birth to him. It is interesting to note that her son Tim, is now the age that she was when she gave birth to him.'

The body never forgets. Once spoken the parallels are indeed clear to see. It explains so much of why I was so driven to succeed and do well at work.

Despite the hiccups and with the help of the counsellor, I got off to a good start with my new client.

This period of calm was cut short when life threw up a very tangible reason to be anxious. My flat was burgled. The burglars came in through the front door and went out through the bedroom window. The police warned they would be back again, this time in through the bedroom window unless I fitted bars. As you can imagine, my previous fears of intruders and me coming to harm, only heightened my anxiety. As far as I was concerned this was no way to live, it was time to leave the capital city. I had wanted to move back to Bath, to be closer to my parents for some time but work always coming first had pushed these plans aside. Despite all the history, it was still a safe place for me. It was familiar. Right now that was what I felt I needed.

Gaining agreement at work for my move was problematic but I was adamant. I had only just started working with my new client and the director who had appointed me was mad as hell with me. I had to escalate my request to move right to the top of the company in order to make it happen. Luckily for me the branch manager at Bristol was looking for an account manager on a huge project involving 10 different airline companies from around the world. Within 48 hours of being matched to this I was on my way.

I bought a house a couple of miles from the centre of Bath. I loved it and the prospect of making it into a real home. I was very happy on my own. All my fears and phobias had receded, and it was a time of great peace.

My house was mid terrace. My closest neighbour, Jan, was a single mum. She had been a few years older than me when she became pregnant and was fortunate to have the full support of her mum. It had still been a very hard road for her, especially before her mum stepped in, and she was put under severe pressure to relinquish her child – essentially being told it was not normal for an unmarried woman to want to keep her child and consequently a sign that she was not well mentally. Hard to believe now, but I understand it was common practice at one time.

Jan and I became firm friends. If our busy work lives allowed we would pop in to see the other during the week. Our respective friends became our joint friends; they were a somewhat eclectic bunch with varied backgrounds and experiences in life, but it worked. On Sunday evenings we would take in it turns to cook for each other but always eat in Jan's house watching TV. We both liked David Suchet, not long into his role as Agatha Christie's detective, Hercule Poirot.

I have always been in great admiration of Jan and of her mum for sticking by her. It was wonderful to see Jan's son grow up, though it tore at my heartstrings as his name is Tim. Tim, the name I had given my son. Every time I looked at him, it took me back to my own loss. Like watching a movie, it gave me a glimpse of what life might have been for me, had my son and I not parted. It was both wonderful and at times, agony.

Jan's Tim was growing into a fine young man. I felt a warm and special connection to him as I saw in him what I would have wanted for my own child. He was a bright, decent and kind human being. And I am delighted to say I was able to help him secure his first corporate job, assisting him to build a successful career for himself.

I miss Jan. We kept in touch for many years after I moved away, but somehow after she herself moved away from Bath our paths parted. I often wonder how she is. I remember Tim getting married, so maybe she is a grandmother now. I have such fond memories and feel privileged to have been her neighbour and friend.

Living in Bath was also a very healing time for my relationship with Mum and Dad and one that I look back on with great love and gratitude. Although the elephant in the room was never addressed and certainly never discussed, I felt closer than ever to them both.

My parents' home, the cottage where I had lived in my teenage years, was about 30 minutes away and they would often drive over for the day. Dad helped me renovate and decorate the house and Mum helped make the furnishings.

While I was without a kitchen installed and all my belongings still in storage, we would go for lunch at a local garden centre. It was a lovely time in my life. Although unspoken, I felt my parents helping me with my house was part of them trying to make things up to me. I basked in the acceptance and returned that love. Once I was settled in, we would see each other every week. I would call by their house for a cup of tea and a natter on my way home from work. Everything felt so good; we were back to a warm and loving family life with lots of laughter.

But with hindsight, I think it also fed into a less healthy narrative. During my formative teenage years I had been harshly rejected and in my opinion, abandoned in my hour of need. This had affected my development and transition from a child to an adult. Ever since retaking my A levels and starting on my journey back to approval, I'd been running on high octane fuel wanting to be the Michelle who would be 'acceptable' to everyone around me.

I was this strange mix. I struggled in intimate social settings and had a dread of unfamiliar places. I'd also become a great people-pleaser in order not to draw disapproval from anyone – from my parents to the people I worked with. I always assumed people were judging me at a personal level and I was desperate that they would not find me wanting. At the same time I was super confident at work, especially when I was leading the way, happy to take anyone or anything on, even if this meant short term displeasure.

At work I fought to have my voice heard. I had this innate belief in my abilities to deliver results that would enable my success. A work colleague once described me as someone who would take 'a tiger by the tail'. At times I was a force to be reckoned with.

Yet in my personal life, I doubted my own ability to make 'the right decisions'. I would run just about everything past my parents to make sure that it would keep me on an even keel with them. Michelle the adult making her own personal decisions in life just did not exist. Living in Bath with my parents so close by only added to this dynamic.

From the moment I gave Baby Tim up for adoption to my moving back to Bath I had managed to do all the things in life that ticked the right boxes with Mum and Dad to such an extent that I was even reinstated in their will. I don't know exactly when this happened and I never did find out what the 'pregnancy penalty' had been. Maybe I was reinstated after my sister died, or maybe when I got my first-class honours degree. Whenever it happened, I was now doing so many things that were acceptable to my parents that they would spend a great deal of time singing my praises to anyone who would listen. They were so proud of me it would burst out from within them. What a saga – here I was busting a gut to achieve things that would make me lovable and acceptable in their eyes, while all the time having the sense that I was leading someone else's life.

It is fair to say that I really enjoyed what I was doing with work. I also loved where things were with me and my parents and the depth of love between us. But, when they went on and on about how great things were in terms of my achievements and their pride in me, I would feel so bleak inside.

It was really strange. I wanted to be happy, my love of my work and achievements was genuine. But no matter what I did I had this dreadful sense of loss and pain. It always got in the way of happiness, or even contentment being possible. The experience of loss and pain remained no matter what I did or didn't do. It was as if part of me was missing and I was constantly searching for – but never finding – anything that could fill this void.

Chapter Twenty-Eight

Every year in sales if you had successfully made your targets you were invited to the '100% Club'. Several hundred sales people and a few nominated technical and administrative staff would jet off to a sunny location. During the day you were expected to attend presentations but there was also a lot of free time. It was seen as a jolly and for the majority this meant drinking alcohol at every opportunity. However, there were always a few who preferred to avoid this. I was one of them. As we headed off to Seville I found myself part of a small group who wanted to make the most of the historical sights Seville had to offer, such as the world-famous Alcazar palace and the beautiful cathedral.

Stephen, a technical specialist, made a welcome addition to our little group, especially for me, as there was a spark between us – literally at one point when our hands brushed against each other. At the end of each evening, he would gallantly offer to walk me and my roommate Ann back to our hotel. The three of us would sit in the hotel lobby, surrounded by the cacophony of sound from several hundred drunken men, made all the more hilarious with Ann and I sharing a pot of tea and Stephen having a coffee.

Back in the UK again, I found I suddenly needed answers or advice on several technical subjects as an excuse to seek Stephen out. When the work was done, we always found time for a chat about anything and everything and before long, we started to see each other outside the office too. We decided it would be best to keep that quiet, not knowing how our colleagues might respond to our blossoming romance. I was used to worrying about the opinions of others. I was used to keeping secrets. But this was a secret that would not stay hidden long.

The Christmas after we first met, Stephen and I decided to go away together. We were still keeping our relationship private but when I told my manager where I would be spending the holidays, he quickly cottoned on. I was going to be in exactly the same place as Stephen. He made the connection.

'Are you seeing each other?' he asked, before anxiously adding. 'What have I said about him in front of you?'

Despite my worries, my manager didn't mind at all that Stephen and I were in a relationship. His biggest concern was that he might have been indiscreet about Stephen in my earshot. He also seemed a little confused.

'But you and Stephen, you're so different,' he said, fluttering his hands to represent two birds flying straight past one another in the sky.

'It's our magnetic personalities,' I replied, laughing to myself as I could see my reference to the science of magnets was too obscure for him.

Stephen and I are very different, it's true, yet there are a great many ways in which we complement each other. Spending time with him felt easy right from the start and after a decade of protecting myself from another heartbreak such as I'd experienced with Ian, I began to think that I might at last be able to let down my guard and let someone in.

That said, I think it was hard for Stephen in the early days as I needed constant reassurance that I was ok, that we were ok and that how I was behaving was ok. See a pattern here? Like any relationship, we would have many ups and downs. However, I quickly learned that Stephen is full of integrity – a man of his word, honest and trustworthy – and he related to me in a way that enabled me to grow in confidence in myself and in our relationship. And, most importantly he is someone who loves me as I am. He values me as me and in doing so enables me to be authentic without fear of judgement.

It was relatively early in our relationship when I told Stephen about my son and the adoption. Stephen's reaction was full of true empathy and compassion.

'That must have been very difficult for you,' he said.

The simplicity of the sentiment and the lack of judgement therein reassured me that I had made the right choice in opening up to him. Here was someone I could trust to understand the magnitude of what I was telling him and not use my secret against me, spreading it like cheap gossip as my former work friend had done.

I loved living in Bath and spending time with Stephen. The only trouble I had, which was still not under control despite the earlier counselling, was the extent to which I was still driven to succeed. I was in a work environment that demanded a pound of flesh and I had delivered plenty. I was still in sales and whatever target the tech giant set I met and exceeded, nine years in a row, bringing in a massive amount of business. The problem was I was completely exhausted.

For some time I had recognised this. I asked to be moved out of sales at the end of every year. Each time I was persuaded to do 'one more year'. As I entered year 10, nothing changed except that I was assigned a new client right in the middle of a tough competitive campaign. Once again I rose to the challenge and closed the business. However, things were really active in this account and no sooner had the deal 'been done' another significant situation needed to be dealt with. Once again, I made it and yes, you know what's coming next, there was another situation brewing that needed to be dealt with in a short time frame.

Suddenly, I lost my capacity to cope. I was so physically and mentally tired. I was dragging myself out of bed each morning and crying a lot of the time. Not that anyone saw any of this at work – there I was still able to maintain the impression that I was handling it all.

I remember one day in particular I had to go about 50 miles to the client offices to collect a signed contract. I was feeling so bad that Stephen drove me there and back. I spent most of the journey in tears. I am not sure what the client thought as I must have looked awful. That was the point at which I decided that I had to go to my GP. He immediately signed me off for a few weeks. My perception of the culture at work meant that stress was not something I wanted on a medical certificate, but thankfully my doctor explained he didn't have to reveal the nature of my health situation to my employer when signing me off.

After being signed off, I spent most of the first couple of weeks in tears and just stayed at home. It was early December and the local dogs home was inundated with dogs. They had asked for foster carers in the local paper, obviously hoping that these would end up providing permanent homes. I went to see them and agreed to take on a dog for six weeks, making it 100% clear that this would only be a temporary arrangement. The nice thing was that this meant I had to get up and out to walk the dog. That really helped. Six weeks later I decided I was ready to go back to work, despite my GP's advice to stay off for longer – something I wish I had listened to for no other reason than it would have been good for me. But back then, I was still the driven me and going back to work was my main focus. The pain and loss and sense of something missing deep within me was still there. Work was the only way I knew how to plaster over the wound.

Back in the office, at last it was agreed I could move out of sales and into sales training. The sales college was in Hampshire and I was able to take up a post there via a secondment. At the same time, Stephen accepted another job role which was also based in Hampshire. We decided to buy a house together and moved in August.

Change is something that triggers my fears and phobias, especially if that change takes me into unknown territory. I was perfectly ok in my new job while I still had my house in Bath, an anchor of familiarity. During the week I had been staying at the college or in Stephen's house and at weekends we stayed at Stephen's place or mine depending on what we were doing.

Once we moved it was a different story. The panic attacks came back. I developed a phobia about being out and about that manifested itself in a different way from my previous experiences. Driving down the little lanes between work and our house was a nightmare for me, especially as the nights drew in. I was completely spooked. It felt as if the trees and hedges on each side of the road were crashing in on me and I could hardly make it home without feeling that I was going to pass out at the wheel.

This time I did go to see my GP promptly and I was referred to the local mental health unit. From here I was invited to take part in a nurse-led change management course which was probably CBT-based, although it was not called that. I am not sure the course helped. I have a feeling it was simply the passage of time and the unfamiliar becoming familiar that led to a reduction and then removal of this phobia. That is certainly how it had always been for me, ever since my teenage experiences, with most new situations I find myself in.

I stayed at the training centre for about 18 months. During this time I gave a lot of thought to deciding what I wanted to do next. Before I moved into this new education role I had considered leaving the company. They had asked for volunteers for redundancy. However, given my physical and mental state and lack of training skills, the secondment made more sense. It gave me time to recover and time to build some relevant experience. I thought this meant I was saying goodbye to the opportunity to leave with money but luckily for me there were several redundancy programmes and I was able to take one.

I was very clear about what I wanted to do and how my training business would work. However, the advisors at the outplacement service were less than encouraging. My ideas did not fit their model and I got fed up with them telling me that my business would never get off the ground. It would fail. Most of their comments seemed to stem from my inability and refusal to shoehorn my business plan into their template, which I thought added no value. So off I went on my own.

Chapter Twenty-Nine

1994/1995

In my own business everything was just up to me. It was up to me to research the markets, decide on my products and services, build and shape these to individual client needs, manage their delivery and deal with all the aspects of what went on with the customer and behind the scenes. It gave me a great sense of freedom – a space to express myself and bring all my creativity and talents to the table. I was shaping my own destiny and I loved it! I was very driven, maybe even more so because it was my business, perhaps even 'my baby', some might say, as I nurtured its growth. And, unlike my experience with the Stock Exchange project, there was no-one to take this away from me,

Despite all the insecurities and uncertainties in my personal life I had complete faith in myself when it came to work. I may have not been fit to be a mother, but I was fit to succeed here. Although I had no big company brand behind me, I knew I was excellent at what I did. I quickly built up a strong client base with several household names clients. So much so that I regularly ended up with more work than was reasonable to handle.

Although this would often lead to me being completely exhausted, it suited me. I loved what I was doing and was gaining genuine enjoyment from my work. Equally I think it was also the perfect way to stop me from having to deal with the emotional devastation that, far from subsiding, was still growing inside of me. I needed to find a way to stop it from surfacing into something that I knew could overwhelm me.

I also knew that I had to do everything I could to open up a pathway for my son to reach me. Tim was now over the age of 18. My biggest hope in life was that when he was of age, he would come looking for me and that we would be reunited.

So far this had not happened.

In 1995, I joined NORCAP. NORCAP was the National Organisation for Counselling Adoptees and Parents (UK), created by Pam Hodgkins MBE, a social worker who is herself an adoptee. The organisation held a register, to which adoptees and birth parents could add their names if they wished to be put in contact with one another.

While thanks to the Adoption Act of 1975, adoptees over the age of 18 were allowed to know details of their birth family's identities if they so desired, the same was not true in reverse. As a birth mother, I was not permitted to know the names of the couple who had adopted my baby or to what his name had been changed. The only way I could have contact with my son post-adoption was if he agreed to be put in touch with me. The NORCAP register was designed to facilitate that process.

I sent a letter, asking to sign up. Reading it again more than 25 years later, my sadness jumps off the page. I wrote:

'I would also like to explore the possibilities to talk with other people who have been through the same experience. Despite it being 23 years now since my baby was adopted, I am finding it hard to come to terms with it

all. If anything it is getting harder as the years go by, especially since he reached the age of 21 and yet no contact has been made. Whilst I realise that he may never contact me, I would like to do everything I can to make sure that the path to me is easy to follow.'

For a couple of weeks, I was in a state of anxious excitement as I waited to hear whether there was a match. Alas there wasn't. My son Tim, now an adult, had not put himself on the Norcap register. All I could do – at least all I thought I could do – was continue to wait and hope.

Chapter Thirty

When I set up my own learning and development company, I knew it would involve a lot of travel to clients around the country and abroad. This was going to be a big problem given I still found it so difficult to go anywhere new on my own. For the first couple of years it was manageable thanks to Stephen, who was always at the end of the phone ready to reassure me that he could come and get me if necessary.

As resourceful as ever, I could see another solution: my friend and colleague Linda. I asked her to travel with me to the workshop locations, to help me set up and clear away at the beginning and end of each day. Her travelling with me and sharing my hotel room meant that I was then calm and fear free.

It worked for Linda, too, as at that time she was caring for her mother-in-law. Being away gave her a break. At first I did not explain my needs, but when I realised that Linda thought I was doing her a favour, I decided she deserved the truth. It was still hard for me to share what was going on for me. Having had to pretend for so long that I hadn't even had a baby, it was ingrained in me never to share my vulnerability at this level. I was very lucky that she is such a good friend and was happy to be my minder!

On those occasions when I was working with an associate, as long as we were travelling together, I had an inbuilt solution without having to share any personal stuff. The only challenges I had to overcome were any bits of travel where our journeys did not overlap. None of this removed the panic 100% but it did help. I often worked in Manchester and thanks to Linda's support I could manage a day trip there on my own as the journey became familiar. I also cultivated the friendship of a couple of local cabbies – Colin to take me from the client to Manchester Piccadilly and Bob to take me to and from the train station at home. I needed to be certain to see a familiar face and they are both such lovely people.

I still had moments of panic. For example, sometimes when travelling back to Hampshire, I would find that I was the only person in the carriage after dark between Reading and Basingstoke. That meant 30 minutes of blind fear. No matter how familiar the route, it was (and still is) challenging for me to travel alone. However, I developed a strategy to deal with this. I got Bob to pick me up from Reading instead of Basingstoke – problem solved.

Dealing with the unexpected was more of a problem. One day I was visiting a client in Manchester. Looking forward to my day, as we approached the station, I rang ahead to say I'd be there in 30 minutes. After arriving at Piccadilly I always took the Eccles tram out towards Salford Quays. This was a relatively easy journey for me as I had completed it several times. Linda had also done the trip with me so that the route had even been familiar to me when I first did it alone. On this particular day I got down to the tramline only to see a notice saying that the trams were suspended.

Without stopping to read the notice in full I went into a blind panic and I was frozen to the spot. How on earth was I going to get out to Salford Quays? Buses were out of the question as I didn't know the routes and my local taxi driver was still doing his school runs.

I know it must seem absolutely bizarre – here I was, a successful business person who came across to clients as competent and unfazed by everything, frozen to the platform at nine in the morning unable to make a simple journey by any other method than the tram I knew. What reason could I give for not arriving, given that I had called from the train to say that I was on time?

I don't know what would have happened if I had not then noticed the small print that listed the Eccles trams as an exception to the suspension. Luckily my tram turned up and I completed the journey.

But I arrived feeling like a physical wreck. Luckily I was well used to being a chameleon and put on a brave face. After all, I had had years of practice showing one thing to the outside world and feeling quite another inside – having my son adopted and not being able to show or discuss how I felt about it, I was a master at this skill set. Arriving and looking cool, calm and collected after this kind of incident was child's play to me.

There are so many other incidents that I could cite but I will pick out just one: this time a journey home from Manchester was interrupted by our train breaking down. I was travelling with my associate and great friend Julia, but she was leaving the train an hour before me. I was being picked up at Basingstoke and with my planned arrival time of 7pm, I thought I would be OK. It would still be daylight. Now with the breakdown, the situation had changed. After making it to Birmingham with many stops and starts we were taken off the train and told we would need to wait a couple of hours for a replacement service. I realised we were going to be very late indeed. I had no confidence that my journey onward from Oxford would be without further incidents, or what time I would arrive at Basingstoke. I was not going to be able to cope. Time for a strategy.

'Where are you travelling to?' I asked the other passengers as I wandered up and down the platform, pausing whenever I heard they were going to Bournemouth or Basingstoke.

'Would you like to team up? There's a few of us going that far and we're travelling together as a group?'

Having earmarked who would be travelling at least as far as Basingstoke, I set off to find a member of staff who could make a decision. By chance I spoke to the person who was going to be the guard on our replacement train. Julia and I were the only two with first class tickets, but I persuaded the guard to let everyone in the group I had gathered together travel in the first-class carriage as we had had such a horrendous journey.

Julia and I always travelled with a load of food. With this and the vouchers given out because of the delay, we had a picnic and a party. I also made sure that everyone in the group had a means to get home, either by the taxis laid on through Virgin or by my husband giving them a lift when he picked me up. The upside for me was that I had generated a strategy which meant I would not be travelling alone late at night after Julia got off at Oxford.

To this day Julia just thinks this was the 'mother hen' in me rounding up people to be helpful and supportive to them during a terrible journey. While I hope I did help them and supported them so that it was a win/win situation, my prime motivation was my need to find a way to cope with the unexpected, without sharing my inner turmoil or descending into blind panic and fear.

The incident shows just how much I always kept inside, hidden from even my closest friends. I lived my life with a cortisol flooded, hyper-vigilant brain and as a result I decided that it was better to pick up a group of strangers – some of whom might have been unpleasant – than to have to face the unknown alone.

I got through everything in ways that didn't require me to explain what I was experiencing to anyone, but it took an enormous amount of energy and eventually in 2008, just around the time of the financial crash, I'd had enough. I'm surprised I lasted that long as will become evident when I detail what happened over the years leading up to that point. I'm just pleased that eventually I recognised the need to first curtail and then stop taking on any business that required me to travel or stay away from home. Not easy when most of my clients had offices around the country.

Back in the second half of the 90's I was already working too hard and using up a lot of energy to deal with my travel issues while recognising that my 'suppress everything' strategy was catching up with me.

As time went by, not hearing from my son was eating me up. My NORCAP letter was languishing in its file, unread. What if my son Tim was no longer alive? What if I never saw him again? All of this was outside my control. I had to sort myself out.

Although at this time, the full extent of my memory loss was not clear to me – I didn't know what I didn't know at that time – I decided to try and fill-in a few of the blanks I knew were there. I decided to go back to St Anne's, in the hope that actually standing in front of the old building, or perhaps even going inside if I was allowed, would stir up some kind of recollection that might help me start to deal with the pain of relinquishing my child.

I travelled to Chepstow and found the building where I had spent those sad strange weeks in 1971 and 1972, but if I was hoping that my memory – particularly my memory of my time with Baby Tim – would come back in a rush, I was to be disappointed.

The building was nothing like I thought. It was no longer a mother and baby home but when I explained the reason for my visit, I was able to go inside. Apparently, I was not the first. No memories were triggered and it all seemed so alien to me. I was sure I remembered being able to see Chepstow Castle from the building but couldn't see, as I looked out from the windows so many years later, how that could ever have been possible.

A short while afterwards, I told Mum and Dad that I had gone back to take a look at the house that had been the mother and baby home. I have no idea why I was telling them this or what led me to try to have the conversation.

'Why didn't you tell us you were going?' responded my mother, before turning to my father and telling him as he walked into the room.

Something inside me snapped. I was telling my mother something so important yet I felt as if the phrase 'why didn't you tell us you were going' made it sound like I had just told her I'd popped to Sainsbury's for a pint of milk. I felt my parents had no understanding of the depth of feeling and the emotions that were whirling around inside me; the things I had been told to keep secret. I remember getting angry and just blurting out, 'I don't think you realise just how awful it's been for me. We've never discussed what happened.'

My tone was emotionally charged as I continued, 'Can you imagine for one minute what it's been like having to act as if I've never had a child!'

As I spoke, I knew my voice was getting louder and my rage becoming more apparent. Mum burst into tears.

'The only reason we've never mentioned it is because we didn't want to upset *you*!' she cried.

Mum crying and becoming distressed herself resulted in me backing off and we went back to not talking about things. I felt it was necessary to rein myself in as I knew that when she cried it was my fault. It only ever happened because I had done something wrong. In fact, her never talking about the situation because it might upset me suddenly felt like my fault. As always, I felt responsible. I should not have raised the subject myself. But now I couldn't take it back and I felt so guilty seeing how it had turned out.

Chapter Thirty-One

Sadly a couple of years after Stephen and I moved in together and not long after I had set up my own company, Mum became very ill. Dad was worried as he had noticed she had a lump and he told me. However, I remember asking Mum about it and her looking me in the eyes and categorically denying it. She had decided not to tell anyone or go to the doctor. Some time later Mum collapsed, unable to breathe, and was taken to hospital.

The pleural space on both of Mum's lungs were full of fluid. About three litres in total were taken off. The lump that Dad told me about was a tumour in one breast that was about the size of my fist and considered inoperable. At the hospital, I was told that Mum would almost certainly be dead within a month and that she was far too ill and past the point of considering chemotherapy or radiotherapy. At that time Mum was a smoker but the doctors even told me not to bother hassling her about this, as there was no point. Not now.

However, Mum was not ready to give up and neither was I. I spent the next 48 hours researching the literature with great energy and devising a strategy to see if a difference could be made. This included Mum taking around a dozen supplements a day. I tried everything I could and eventually the supplements seemed to make a difference. This spurred us on further. To everyone's astonishment, Mum improved to the point that the doctors offered her chemotherapy.

No-one in the medical profession ever explained to us that the chemotherapy was palliative in nature. Mum went ahead and I have to say that although the sessions she managed to endure were tough on her to the point that she could not complete all six, it did seem to help. The tumour began to shrink, her lymph nodes responded and after the chemotherapy was stopped she managed to live a relatively normal life for over a year. Then, horror of horrors, in addition to her tumour advancing again another tumour developed in the other breast. This was a different cancer type. So now she had one oestrogen positive tumour and one oestrogen negative one.

Years later, I read how the treatment used to block oestrogen receptors can cause this situation, but back then it was considered unusual. Another course of chemotherapy and radiotherapy followed. Once that was completed there was only a short interval before things started to go downhill again and another four sessions with a third combination of drugs was introduced. A total of 12 chemotherapy sessions with three different combinations of drugs and radiotherapy really took its toll; not helped by septicemia, MRSA and other infections such as Candida that were picked up along the way. The third set of chemo drugs also damaged Mum's heart.

All of this took place over a four-year period. To the day Mum died she was of the opinion that any breath was better than no breath. She so wanted to live. Anyone looking at her may have wondered what quality of life she had – at the end she weighed just five stone and was unable to walk – but she still wanted to fight on. I was with her every step of the way.

Towards the end of Mum's life, I worked hard to make sure she was properly cared for, I travelled between Hampshire and Bath as often as I was able. I moved heaven and earth to be her advocate. As a result of the events that had led up to my sister Anna's untimely death, Mum had a deep distrust – and fear – of doctors and hospitals. I never let her face that fear alone. If she had a GP or hospital appointment, I would be there. If she had to stay in overnight, I would stay too, sleeping in a chair if I had to.

I slept in a lot of strange places – the floor in sister's office in the NHS hospital, chairs in corridors or at my mother's bedside. On better days, I stayed at my dear friend Maria's house. I also lived on a really poor diet – hospital canteen food or microwaved meals that I could eat on the ward. In addition, the travel back and forth between my house and the hospital where both my parents were being treated or to my parents' house was not easy.

My life was really unsettled – I managed to keep the business going via my great network of associates. That came at a price though, as I was paying out most of what I was charging the clients and for at least one year, the year leading up to Mum's death, it meant I operated at a loss. Not that it mattered though; the business was kept going ready for me to pick up the reins again. Generally my clients were supportive. I hope they recognised the lengths I went to in order to ensure their business needs and my commitments to them were covered. Looking back now I am absolutely amazed at how well human beings can cope when they really have to. The energy and capacity to do so just came from somewhere.

Dad also had his role – he was Mum's carer at home. Without him it would have been impossible for her to stay at the house. He did a splendid job 24/7 even after he was diagnosed with cancer himself. He cooked, he cleaned, he took Mum out and he managed all her personal care with such love.

Dad's own cancer must have made it difficult. It was also hard for him coping when Mum was in hospital, as the house was in a remote location and my parents always worried about it being left empty – hence he would go home every night and I would stay at the hospital or nearby.

I remember one awful night when Mum was quite close to dying and Dad just collapsed at her bed side. He had dashed home to check on the house and then come back. I think the strain of it all and perhaps finally accepting that she was soon going to die just caught up with him. The whole thing was almost a comedy sketch if it hadn't been so sad – I had staff from A&E dragging Dad by his feet across the floor out of the room and trying to do this in a way that would not alarm my mother.

Later on, I had Dad's anger to handle as he was so upset that I had called staff in to deal with him. This was all pretty close to the end after a three-week stint of my mother being in hospital.

The last time we waited in A&E for Mum to be admitted I was determined that she would have a bed on the cancer ward. I refused any other available beds, which was a strategy that Mum's consultant had recommended to me in advance of our arrival. Mum was expected to die shortly (a frequent admission expectation over the 4 years) and I was not going to allow her to be dumped in an inappropriate ward. This was something that had happened to us too many times before. Eventually not only did we make it onto the cancer ward but she was allocated a single room.

During the next few days Mum wanted to talk about dying with Dad but he could not do this. His coping strategy was to continually tidy the room which used to drive me nuts! Eventually Mum gave up trying to have a discussion with him and she told me that she wanted to be cremated. When I said this to Dad, he went ballistic as he had strong views that this was something that Mum should only talk to him about – a bit of a catch 22 situation given his refusal to discuss things.

Mum died on a Friday afternoon of a Bank Holiday weekend. Sadly I was not in the room as I had gone to get something to eat, but both Dad and my sister were there. I remember a sense of relief though, as I was beginning to think that none of us were going to be able to cope with the intensity of the situation, lack of sleep and constant bed-side vigil for very much longer. I did know that Mum was going to die very soon. Earlier in the week she had been given a self-administering pump. She and I had understood that this was to administer Valium to help take the edge off of her anxiety – why, oh, why we thought that I have no idea? We discovered that it was morphine.

Mum and I had discussed that she needed to take care with morphine because of its effects on the respiratory system. She had been taking Oramorph for some time before being admitted, as the cancer was now in her bones. She well knew that if she said she was still in pain and the dose was increased there would come a point when she would stop breathing. Earlier that day she had asked the doctor 'what else could he do to cure her?' and 'Was he absolutely sure that there was nothing else?'

I think that after finally accepting the doctor's answer that everything possible had been done, this was it. Mum wanted to go. She then started to mention how much pain she was still in and her distress was evident. She started saying that if she knew how bad things were she would have wanted to go earlier. She was probably referring to the whole situation, the doctors and nurses assumed she was referring to the pain she was in at that time. Extra morphine was offered. Before this was given I remember checking in with her. 'Are you really sure this is what you want?' I asked.

Chapter Thirty-One

She and I both knew what I was talking about even if Dad and Christine didn't.

'Yes,' she answered.

I then told her that I loved her very much and she replied that she loved me too. I knew then that she understood fully what was going to happen, if not that day, then some time very soon, and that it was what she wanted.

How do I know that Mum was ready to go? Well, whenever I had told Mum that I loved her, her automatic reply was always 'it goes without saying'. Somehow the words 'I love you' or 'I love you too' were outside her usual vocabulary. When she actually replied with those words, I knew they would be the last we ever said to each other. A little while later she drifted off to sleep and I went to get something to eat.

When I returned she had died.

Although Mum and I never discussed anything to do with my pregnancy or the adoption in any depth – our conversation about my visit to St Anne's had convinced me that was impossible – the four years we spent together during her illness was a very rich experience for me. I think it was also the same for her. We came to understand, accept and respect each other in a way that had been absent until then. And we shared something that is inexplicable.

A few days before Mum died, I experienced a passing of energy or life force from her to me. It had such strong physical (heat) and mental elements to it. I really can't describe or explain it. All I do know, is that for many years afterwards I could still 'feel' her within me. And then one day she left me – it was time for her to go, to move on, and it was ok.

I am really pleased that I was there to take care of her in the way that I did. I see it as one of the biggest achievements in my life. And, I think me taking care of her to the extent that I did also meant a lot to her too – she certainly told me that it did, which in itself was something very special. The last few years leading up to Mum's death were such a healing time for us. When she died, we were both at peace with one another absolutely.

Chapter Thirty-Two

My father was devastated by Mum's death. Although he tried very hard to carry on living I think he was just too sad.

My sister Christine and I turned our focus to him, making sure that one or the other of us visited Dad each week. Christine had been living abroad for most of Mum's illness but she had moved back to England and invited Dad to come and live with her and her family. Much as I think he wanted to live with Christine, especially with her boys, Dad expected to live with me as the eldest. That was the way things worked. But I was not forthcoming with an offer.

I felt caught between Stephen and Dad. Stephen had put a lot of time in driving me to and from the hospital when I was exhausted and sitting around to keep me company. It must have been very hard for him in the four years leading up to my mother's death and beyond that with my father. I'm sure he felt neglected as I was so caught up with them. But, as always, he was there for me.

Despite my best efforts to support him, Dad and I seemed to be constantly at odds. It was a difficult set of circumstances. His cancer was progressing at speed and his grief was so intense. His wife, the person whom he had adored and cherished for so many years had gone. It was challenging for him to gather strength to carry on. At the same time, I had lost my mother after an intense time together. I was not at my best. Somehow in the cycle of grief for both of us, past resentments began to surface. Knowing that I might soon lose him, too, I wanted to find a way to make my peace with Dad, especially in connection with my baby Tim. I wanted him to die knowing that we were OK.

My solution to the problem was a radical one and there was no guarantee that it would work. I decided that the best way to heal my relationship with Dad would be to ask him to help me in my search for my son.

I suggested that Dad write to the adoption agency that had arranged Baby Tim's placement, to ask if they had any information on my son that they might be able to share. Dad did as I asked, then we waited. Given that I'd been on the Norcap register for five years without hearing anything whatsoever, you could have knocked me down with a feather when the agency wrote back in short order, telling me and Dad that they could act as intermediary and contact my son on my behalf.

This news was very welcome but also very confusing. I realised that I had not expected it to be so easy. What about all the things I had been told about not having any rights? That the best I could hope for was that my son would initiate a search for me? I expected Dad's letter to receive a polite, non-committal reply. But no, the agency was actually offering to help. They knew who had adopted my son. They knew where to find him and they were happy to reach out and ask whether he would like to hear from me. It was as though I had been pushing against a locked door for 28 years – and it had suddenly swung open, leaving me to fall right through it.

'Yes, yes, yes... please ask him,' I pleaded as the tears streamed down my face.

I was fearful and scared, yet amazed at the situation presented to me.

This was really deep stuff, as in addition to the possibility of being reunited with my son, I knew that Dad was dying and from somewhere within me came this desire to give him a chance to make his own peace with his grandson.

I hadn't up until then given any thought to how the adoption might have affected my father. In my eyes, even at that moment and for a long time after, he was one of the villains of the piece – one of the people who had stopped me from keeping my son. He had told me through his words and actions (such as changing the terms of his will) that I was a very bad girl, tainted and unlovable unless I behaved in 'acceptable ways'. All these years we had never really discussed anything about the pregnancy or the adoption in either a factual or emotional way.

Yet here I was, either acting as the dutiful daughter, or as the genuinely compassionate daughter who wanted to close the circle and put things right for Dad before he died. I have no idea which person I was actually being, as my decades-long fabrication of one person within another was so complete that even I could not distinguish genuine behaviours from those that simply elicited a sense of 'being a good girl'. Little did I know how rocky the road between me and Dad was going to be.

One day Dad, still reeling from the death of my mother, put together and handed me a photo album.

'Here we have a record of all our family, something for you and Christine to treasure after I have gone,' he told me.

I sat down and looked through the album with interest. It was full of photos of people I had vaguely heard of but never met, such as my maternal grandmother and grandfather, my father's half-brother and his children. I also saw pictures of my sister and her husband. There were photos of me and my sister as babies and pictures of her children as infants, too. I have given you a clue of what is coming next. Nowhere, absolutely nowhere, in the album was a picture of me with my son, Tim.

In a moment, my father's words about the album being 'a record of all our family' drew out emotions of anger and outrage. Shouting and ranting, I roughly handed it back to him. 'How could you do this? How on earth can it be a complete record of our family when there was absolutely no acknowledgment of me having had a son; your first grandchild?'

A lmost as if I was an observer to the situation, I saw Dad reacting with shock and confusion. He simply did not get what I was saying. I believe he had genuinely not expected any reaction other than pleasure at what he had done.

My poor old dad. He tried to make things better. I actually had some photos of Tim and I with me at the house; photos taken at his christening. I am not sure why – perhaps I had brought them with me as part of preparing to write to the agency. What I do remember is fat being added to the fire by Dad going through my things to find those photos without first asking me. He lifted a couple of them, including one of him with Tim – taken at the baptism – and put them together with a few more photos of other family members into a second smaller album.

Dad then presented this new album to me. There was real pride in his voice as he explained what he had done. It must have been awful for him when, once again, his attempt at a kind gesture was met with anger and ranting.

'How dare you go through my things without my permission! How dare you choose photos and remove them from my collection!' I cried.

I know that he meant well – but in that moment, I was blind to it and all I could do was shout.

In many ways, my actions after this unfortunate incident compounded the situation. I had a dilemma now. Of course I wanted the agency to contact my son for me, but I no longer wanted Dad to be a part of the process. I suddenly wanted to keep all news of any contact and especially any arrangements to meet up completely private. This was my business, my moment in time with my son. I was quite staggered at how strongly I felt and the deep anger and other negative emotions that surfaced as my dream seemed to be closer to coming true.

It was particularly hard for Dad as I had instigated the idea of getting him involved. Now I was taking this involvement away from him and being cagey when he asked me how things were progressing. He must have felt so shut out and hurt. With hindsight I do know that he was trying his best to make things better.

But I also think I was right that this next part of the process did need to be private. Just as my last moment with Baby Tim had been private, I wanted any potential first moment in reunion to be private too.

I told the agency to go ahead and make the connection, then waited anxiously to hear the outcome.

Chapter Thirty-Three

Just as I had been lifted by the news that the agency might be able to connect me with my son, I was floored by the response to their first approach. It was not my son who responded, but his adoptive mother. She telephoned the agency and said that she did not think it was a good idea for me to try to come back into my son's life. She thought that it would be 'unsettling' and asked the agency to ensure that I make no further contact.

When I was told about this, I was so angry. What right did she have to decide on a grown man's behalf whether or not he wanted to meet his birth family? Baby Tim would have been 28 at this point. I began to wonder whether his adoptive mother had opened the letter from the agency and maybe not even told him about the enquiry for contact. My fears were made even worse when she called the agency for a second time, reiterating her thoughts on how undesirable contact would be for her son. This time she asked the agency to pass a message to me – that 'the baby I had given up for adoption had reached his full potential'. What the hell did that mean? Her message baffled me as I had no idea what the phrase 'he has reached his full potential' meant.

Of course, I understand now how frightened Baby Tim's adoptive mother must have been to receive the news that I wanted to be in touch. I wonder if, over the years, she had worried about this very moment. Her calls to the agency seemed to reveal her fears. She wanted me to know that my baby had 'reached his full potential'; the implication being that he would not have been able to do so had he stayed with me. She was telling me that he had done alright without me – better than alright, thanks to her and her husband – so there was no need for me to come crashing back into his life now, or at least that was my perception. The agency's initial enquiry to see if contact was welcomed and the subsequent calls from Baby Tim's adoptive mother might have been the end of it. I'm sure that's what she hoped. Thankfully Carole, the social worker the agency had assigned to me, persevered and said that it was not her decision, as her son – my son – was over 18.

She encouraged me to continue with the contact process and to write a letter for them to forward to Tim. I took my time composing my words, and with genuine care towards both Tim and his adoptive parents, I wrote.

October 1999

I cannot begin to understand what it must be like for you to grow up knowing that you were put forward for adoption when only six weeks old. I have no idea of what has been explained to you or indeed what your thoughts and reactions are towards your adoption or to this letter.

Firstly I want to reassure you that I appreciate that you have your own life with parents who love and care for you a great deal, and that I am just as interested as you in protecting your relationship with them. I realise and accept that they are the ones who have spent days and nights worrying about you, supporting you and caring for you and in every sense of the word they are your parents. *I gave up my rights to sharing those very precious parts of your life when I agreed to your adoption.*

However I always think of you and I will continue to do so. The pain and sadness of parting from you is always there as is my love for you. It's hard to put such deep and complex emotions into words. I will always welcome contact from you, whenever you think it is an appropriate moment in your life.

I wish the very best for you and above all else I hope that you are happy, safe and well.

With love
Michelle

Chapter Thirty-Four

Carole, the agency social worker, was very good. She was very clear that any decision to reunite was my son's and not his adoptive mother's to make. I remember questioning her about this as I was so surprised that I could initiate contact and the lengths that she and the agency went to, to establish if contact was wanted.

I was even more surprised by her saying that the agency was ashamed of their past and were trying to make up for things in the only way they could.

This quiet acknowledgment, albeit informal, was very important to me. For years I had convinced myself that all the pain and grief I'd been through, I had brought entirely upon myself. After all, I had put my signature on the adoption papers. The agency's appeasing actions suggested to me that they knew they hadn't been acting entirely in my best interests after all.

Carole's advice was that whatever happened next, I should be prepared to take things slowly. If Tim did want to be in touch, there was a lot for us to adapt to. Last time we were together we were mother and baby, now we would be meeting as mother and adult son with no shared history of experiences since our separation. It was frustrating, since it added extra time to the process, but I understood why it was the recommended way to approach the situation.

Then came the message from Carole that yes, my son Tim did want us to be in contact. It is impossible to describe fully what it was like for me to hear these words. All I can say is every part of me on every level, including my soul, was ready for this.

We were encouraged to take time to get to know each other. We were advised to start with a letter exchange through the agency and then to progress to a phone call providing we both wanted to move forward. We were also advised to allow time and space between each contact to assimilate and take on board what was happening. Good advice I'm sure but that's just not how things went.

In my first letter to Tim after contact was made I shared information about myself, my interests, my career and so on. The agency's rationale for both of us doing this was that it would help us to adjust to meeting up as two adults. That made sense to me. This time though, rather than writing a letter to be placed in a file with no idea if it was ever going to be seen, I was writing directly to my son.

October 1999

Dear Timothy,

I write to you in this name, as it is the name I gave you when you were born and the only name I know you by. It is also the name of your birth father.

In writing to you now, I want to reassure you that I respect that you have your own life and your relationship with your mum and dad, and that any further communication between us needs to be right for you.

I often think of you and over the years have wondered what life might have been like if I had been able to keep you – possibly very different who knows.

I was 16 when you were born and Tim my boyfriend was a year older. We were both still at school. I went to Bath Convent and Tim to St. Brendan's in Bristol.

I still keep in touch with your birth father, Tim… We have both always thought that it is important for us to keep in touch.

I have no idea if you do want to know about why you were put up for adoption so I have decided to wait until I understand what your thoughts and wishes are. For now I thought that I would simply tell you a bit about my life and give you some background on your birth families. I enclose a photograph of you and me at your christening that took place in the mother and baby home where I stayed. It is my favourite photograph of us together.

As advised by the agency I continued the letter with information, much of which has been covered earlier, that would give Tim a sense of his roots and a little about who I was today and what I was like. I finished the letter by saying:

I hope that you have had a happy time growing up and that you are settled in your life. It is my hope to meet you again one day. As I said before I respect that it all depends on what is right for you and your parents. I do want you to know that although parting from you was the saddest moment in my life I have always treasured giving birth to you. I am so pleased to know that you are safe. I hope that you are happy and well and that hearing from me adds to your life in some way whatever you decide you want to do from here.

With love Michelle

Michelle. It was hard to sign my letter Michelle, when I had once been his 'Mum' but I knew it was the right way to end this first letter.

After I had sent my letter to the agency, I was so excited and scared at the same time. What if he changed his mind or something I had written upset him? I kept in close contact with Carole as I waited for a response.

A short while later, the postman delivered a bundle of mail. I picked it up off the mat and flicked through the little pile, not expecting there would be anything of much interest. Bills, bills, bills... But the moment I saw that handwritten envelope, I knew. My heart was in my mouth and I began to shake. This letter was from my son. It had to be.

I didn't know how he had got my address – such things were not revealed through the mediation service – so my first thought was 'Oh my God, my son is someone I already know! We must have already met'. I cannot begin to tell you how strange these thoughts felt. If we knew each other, did we like each other? Had we already shared time and activities together? But hang on a minute. How many 28-year-old men did I know? Not one to my knowledge.

I sat down and ripped the envelope open. As I started to read, all became clear. I read how he had pieced together all the information that I had given him and searched for me on the Net. Not only that, he was proud of having done so and, you know what, I was proud too. I smiled with pride and thought to myself – that's my boy – here is my first sight of how we are alike. I too would have bucked the system in his shoes. I would have wanted to take control of the situation and my own destiny.

I read that letter again and again. It was fantastic to read about his life. He had certainly excelled himself academically with his doctorate and his career was an interesting one.

Chapter Thirty-Four

I was holding in my hand a piece of paper that my son had held in his. It was the closest I had come to touching him since the moment 28 years earlier, when I thought that he and I were saying goodbye forever.

Chapter Thirty-Five

Reunion quickly presented its own challenges. To begin with, I had to stop thinking of Baby Tim as the infant I'd last held at St Anne's. While my scant memories of him may have been frozen in time, obviously he was not. Likewise, I had to get out of the place in my head where I was still only 16 years old and relate to John, as I now knew him to be called, as an adult. Even getting used to John being called John wasn't easy. Immediately, I began to worry that I would forget and inadvertently call him by his baby name. I'd spent so long thinking of him as my Baby Tim. It was going to be a challenge.

We had to meet each other in the 'here and now'. To help us get to that stage, we swapped more letters and photographs. I pored over the photos John sent me, looking for the baby I had lost in his very grown-up face; looking for family resemblances. He had thick, dark hair, like his father's, but in the shape of his eyes, I thought I could see my own Dad. I imagined how it might have been had he grown up among us, how we would have told him about the echoes of his ancestors that he carried in the way he smiled. I wondered what his adoptive family look like. Did John ever search the faces of the people he had grown up around in this way, hoping to find some commonality? I wondered if he was looking at the photographs of me that I'd sent him, and finding echoes of his own face there.

I guess we must have spoken on the phone at some point, but you know what, I simply don't remember. What I do remember focusing on is preparing to meet up for the first time.

John first made contact towards the end of 1999 but it wasn't until January 2000 that we were able to meet in person. The decision to get together raised all sorts of new questions and worries. Where would we meet? Who would be there?

I felt that our first meeting in reunion needed to be as private and peaceful as the moment we'd said 'goodbye', therefore we should be by ourselves, just the two of us. And it had to take place on a sort of 'neutral ground' – not in my home or John's but somewhere in between. Where could I find somewhere that we could be properly alone for this hugely important moment?

I quickly decided that this momentous event could not be at a pub or hotel, where people might constantly be walking through, observing us in the most private of private moments, potentially making it difficult to be as open and honest as I hoped we would want to be. What if we both burst into tears? I was one hundred percent certain that I would. The last thing we needed was an audience.

Then I had a brainwave. I suddenly thought of Jane Austen's House at Chawton, or Chawton Cottage as it was known when the writer spent the last eight years of her life there. There was no logical thought as to exactly why, but meeting in the house where she wrote *Emma* and *Persuasion* just felt a perfect fit. I went to see the team there, told them my story and asked if I could book a room to meet my son in private. To my delighted surprise, they said they would be very pleased to help. I don't know what prompted such kindness. Perhaps the person who heard my plea had some experience of the pain of being separated from a beloved child. Perhaps they were an adoptee themselves. Whatever the reason, the team at Jane Austen's House offered me the use of the kitchen – a part of the house not open to the public at that time – where John and I could be utterly private, cocooned by history.

It was the perfect solution. I'd been to the house, now a museum, a number of times before and liked the way it felt. I was not a big reader of Austen, unlike Stephen, but I do think that she, more than any other author, understood the power of social mores, the pressures on women to conform and how the need to be seen to be 'respectable' could tear lives apart. I was sure that Ms Austen would have approved of my choice.

As the date for that first meeting drew nearer, I became more and more anxious. So many questions ran through my head: What would John think of me? Did he want to know anything about me or would he just want to know why he had been adopted and whether I was sorry for 'giving him away'? How could I make a good first impression that would encourage him to let me be a part of his life? I remember gathering up more photos of us together and also making a collage of pictures, as advised by the agency, depicting many of the things I had done and places I'd travelled to, despite all my travel challenges with unfamiliar places.

On the day of our meeting, I was as anxious as someone preparing for a life-changing job interview. I stood in front of the mirror, examining myself with a critical eye. I'd never been particularly interested in fashion, preferring jeans and t-shirts to dresses. I dressed smartly for work but was not the kind of woman who wore high heels unless I absolutely had to. If I went out in heels, I would inevitably end up falling over, scuffing them and ripping my tights. I was an outdoor countryside girl by nature. But how did I want John to see me? Was this outfit right? Did I look too trendy? Or too staid? Did I look like someone he would want to be hugged by? Did I look like a mother?

I must have changed clothes at least five times before I settled on the outfit that I thought best represented the 'me' I wanted my son to see. Stephen gave me the thumbs up. He knew how much getting this moment right meant to me. With hindsight, I am not sure I chose well, but equally I am not sure it mattered. It was a bit mumsy. Perhaps that was a good thing. Who knows?

I drove to Chawton alone, arriving early. I wanted to be there first to make sure that everything was in place. I parked up and sat in my car for a moment, trying to gather myself. My heart was hammering in my chest. Almost three decades had passed since I last laid eyes on my child. I would be seeing him again in just a few minutes. It seemed utterly surreal.

Taking a deep breath, I unclipped my safety belt, got out of the car and walked on shaking legs to the front door of the beautiful 17th-century house. A guide was waiting to lead me through the public areas to the warm and cosy kitchen where this magical moment, the one I had waited so long for, was about to happen.

Chapter Thirty-Six

As for the meeting itself, well that gets a little hazy. My strategy in life, perfected over so many years, is to forget anything that stresses me. Not just forget in the sense that I 'forget my keys', but really forget as in 'erase the memory completely from my conscious mind'. Because of this, all I can tell you is that most of my first meeting with John is a complete mystery to me – yet another one of many blank moments in my life.

So what do I remember? I remember wanting to reach out and touch him, wanting to have a physical connection with my son, my baby son, for whom I had yearned for all these years. I felt this overwhelming emotion as I had waited for so long for this and had so many expectations and hopes: we would fall into each other's arms, we would reconnect with an immediate sense that we belonged together. Yet instead, I am faced with a young man who is in effect a stranger to me.

As I write, I am transported back there. I feel the moment is unreal, surreal even. I don't know or understand fully what I feel: a mixture of love from the depths of my soul, yet also confusion, a sense of things whirling in my head trying to land in some kind of rational way. Right now, there is only one moment in time, the past, co-existing with the present, and my tentative hopes for the future.

I look at John, the man who introduces himself as John, John the adult who has written and spoken to me, but there are four people in that kitchen as we meet for the first time since 1972. Despite our best efforts to ensure we were meeting as adults, I brought my 16-year-old self and John came both as adult and as infant, Baby Tim.

And who was my adult self in this context? I hesitate to use the word 'mother' as I am not sure who I am at this point. On the one hand, I feel so connected to John both as my baby Tim and as my adult son, yet at the exact same time, so disconnected too. There is a myriad of confusion at every level – both physically and emotionally. It was so all-consuming.

Our first meeting as adults was filled with all these complexities, yet at the same time it was miraculous and wonderful. I don't know what I said or told John or what he told me or asked. What I can say is this was and still is one of the most precious moments in my life, despite my mind executing its strategy of erasing a lot of specific details.

Talking that afternoon at Jane Austen's House was easy. We had plenty to catch up on after all. But when the time came for us to part again, I was completely thrown. Could I hug him? I wanted to. Thankfully, John was happy to be hugged and held tight.

I think John and I spent less than two hours together on the first day of our reunion. Two hours couldn't begin to make up for the time we'd lost but I knew I had to be careful not to push for too much too soon. I couldn't expect John to want to jump straight back in to a mother-son relationship with me. Though he is part of me, my flesh and blood, in so many ways we were still total strangers to one another. I was not the one who had

had been there throughout his childhood, ready to scoop him up and hug him when he fell and kiss his bumps and bruises better. I wasn't the one who had taught him his manners, or sat and listened to him when he was learning how to read. I wasn't the one who made sure he was well-fed while he did his revision or watched him graduate. I had not been there for so many important moments in his life.

I was pleased however to discover that John's adoptive parents had kept Timothy Peter as his middle names. Perhaps they just liked the names and would have happened upon them themselves anyway, but I liked to think that they kept those names as a way of recognising the little person John already was when they welcomed him into their family. It was a way of linking him to his past. To me.

I drove back home and collapsed onto the sofa. The afternoon had gone very well, but it had left me in a state of emotional overwhelm. I was very grateful that Stephen was there for me when I got back, ready to listen to me talk about the meeting if I wanted to. At the same time, he understood that I would need time alone to let it all sink in.

Years later, I would ask John what he remembered of that day.

'I don't remember much. It's very hazy. It was so over-whelming. There was so much going on,' he admitted.

Chapter Thirty-Seven

If the days leading up to that meeting in the kitchen at Jane Austen's house had been an anxious time, the weeks that followed were agonising. Having finally reunited with my son, of course I wanted to spend more time with him. I wanted to talk to him every day. There was so much I still wanted to tell him and so much I wanted to ask but I had to hold back. I could not bombard him with calls, emails or text messages. I had to wait for him to make the next move.

I wanted to give John time – time and space – to work out how I was going to fit back into his life, if indeed there was a place for me at all. There was also the fact that his adoptive parents did not know that he and I had even spoken to one another. As far as John's adoptive mother, his mum, was concerned, her phone calls to the agency marked the end of it. She'd given me all the information she thought I had the right to know. That John had 'fulfilled his potential'.

Given how strongly his adoptive mother had reacted to that early contact, it's no surprise that John was adamant that he could not yet tell his parents that he and I were now properly in touch. He was worried that they would react badly to the news;

that they would be upset and feel he was rejecting them or that he was ungrateful for all that they had done for him since he was just a few weeks old. The only solution as far as John could see was that I would have to remain a secret.

I had no idea that I would have to remain so for a very long time.

While all this was going on, a really big curve ball arrived on the radar. Stephen had not seemed his usual self for some time. We first became aware of a problem towards the end of 1999. Stephen had always been very fit. I could not keep up with him easily when we were out and about. Then all of a sudden, he lost his aerobic capacity and would get breathless when we were out walking. I was concerned and wanted him to see a doctor, but you know what men can be like when it comes to seeing their GP. Eventually I persuaded him to go.

Twenty-four hours later, our usual GP at the practice called and said he wanted to see Stephen first thing in the morning. Stephen said 'no', explaining that he had a meeting but the GP took a firm line, explaining in no uncertain terms that Stephen *would* be there. We never imagined that Stephen would end up being sent straight from this appointment to hospital for the tests that would reveal he had cancer.

The diagnosis was a bolt from the blue. It was the very last thing we had expected. Faced with such bad news and not yet really knowing what the outcome might be, Stephen and I quickly decided that, after 10 years as a couple and three years of living together, it was time for us to get married.

We came home from the hospital and straight away applied for a special marriage licence. We were booked in at the register office a few days later. The only thing we had to do then was call around to see if our friends were free to join us.

Chapter Thirty-Seven

Though it was unexpected and hurried in the organisation, looking back our wedding was perfect for us. Even if we had got married under what I shall term 'normal circumstances', I would have changed very little. Perhaps I would have dressed up more rather than ask everyone to come as casually as possible (I wore a jumper and jeans). And there were a couple of friends who could not make the date at such short notice. I wish they could have been there. Apart from that, if I was doing it again, I would want to do it the same way – nice and relaxed.

That said, there were moments during our wedding ceremony when I felt I might be overcome with my emotions. On the one hand, Stephen and I were getting married at last. We were making our love for one another official. That was definitely something to celebrate. On the other hand, we were coming together in this most important moment, not knowing what Stephen's prognosis might be. The fact was, he might not have long to live. For that reason, the ceremony was bittersweet and I worried that everyone – me, Stephen and our guests – would be in tears by the time we exchanged rings.

Luckily, among us was our friend Jennie. Jennie's job took her all over the world and often, when she had to go away, we would look after her dog Katie, a springer spaniel cross. We loved having Katie to stay and she loved staying with us. When she was with us in our home, she was part of the family, so I was adamant that she had to be at the wedding too.

One of the most endearing things about Katie was how much she liked to sing. The moment we put music on, she would start howling along. It wasn't always tuneful but it was always enthusiastic. That day, when our wedding ceremony seemed just a little too poignant, I nervously started humming *The Wedding March*. Katie, with her dog's super hearing, picked up on the tune and joined in with great gusto, raising the roof with her joyful howls. Her whole-hearted singing soon had everyone in fits of laughter. I'll always be grateful to her for making our day so special.

My friend Rachel, who is a cordon bleu chef, didn't attend the ceremony but instead went to our house to get the wedding feast ready for when we returned. She did a wonderful job and it was a lovely party.

The next day Stephen and I returned to Basingstoke and spent our 'honeymoon' in the hospital, while Stephen had a blood transfusion, a necessary pre-requisite to his life saving surgery.

I feel so lucky to be married to Stephen. Over time I have come to trust that I am in a relationship with a man who respects and values me for who I am.

At times we laugh though, as Stephen reminisces how long it took him to see the real me with all the hidden facets of my life and how these things would seep out. For example, the first time he learnt that I have terrible challenges with flying (so much that I have been stretchered off a plane in the past) was when we were sitting airside in an airport about to take off for Russia on a trip that was going to take us onward from there to China. Let's just say that by the time we returned home he was well-versed in how I react to getting on or being on planes. Later he discovered the same was true for ferries. I think he is somewhat challenged at times to know where we can go for a holiday!

While Stephen sees the outside things that many others see – the articulate, confident, professional woman who appears to glide through life being able to take just about anything in her stride, that person who would take 'a tiger by the tail', he also sees the inner me. Not only the little things like how I am with planes, but the really deep stuff – the sadness, the turmoil and inner struggles, and just how difficult everything can be for me.

Especially when it comes to the years of separation from my son and the challenges that come from being reunited without any normal shared family history. Not to mention the complexities that come with all the other people who need consideration within that relationship.

Stephen supports me with kindness, compassion and understanding. On a practical side, he is always there to pick me up or be on call to assist. And with the deeper stuff, he just knows when I want him to put his arms around me and when I need space and time to myself. There are no expectations on me of who I need to be or what I need to do to be OK. We are very good together and I am very fortunate to have Stephen in my life.

Chapter Thirty-Eight

At the same time, my father's health continued to deteriorate. I spent my days driving between Stephen's hospital bed in Basingstoke and Dad's house in Bath. As far as Dad was concerned, as the eldest daughter my role was to take care of everything and that's what I did as far as I was able.

While all this was going on, I was still processing the euphoria of reunion. Dad knew that I had met John at Jane Austen's House but had yet to meet him himself. We were sure it would happen and we thought we still had plenty of time. But then Dad, who was already in hospital, was diagnosed with late-stage kidney failure. One of the consultants called me and advised me that I should come to Bath as quickly as I could. It was the call that every one of us dreads receiving. The consultant was basically telling me that Dad did not have long to live.

It was a Saturday. Naturally, I rushed to be by Dad's side, knowing that he would need someone to advocate for him, just as my mother had done before. The consultant, who neither of us had met before, didn't sugar-coat the situation.

'Well Mr, Pearson you are on the train to death, would you like to take the slow train or the fast train?' he said, in front of me.

'Your kidneys have gone into irreversible failure. If we do nothing you will be on the fast train, if we catheterise your kidneys you will be on the slow train. Now here are all the reasons you may like to consider the fast train. Your wife died recently…'

It was a brutal way to have illustrated Dad's 'choices'. Even the male nurse who was in the room at the time seemed shocked. His jaw was practically on the floor. I was flabbergasted. I could not believe what I had heard. I asked the consultant to leave us and sat with my dad while he took in the information.

Having weighed up his options, Dad chose to have no further treatment, deciding against painful interventions that might at best gain him only a few more weeks of life. It was a terrible moment, but I knew that I should not try to persuade Dad otherwise. He had accepted his fate and I had to accept his choice. He was moved into a side room, where he would be given palliative care.

But Dad's decision had left me with a really big dilemma. Since my first meeting with John, I had convinced myself that I could not call him but had to wait for him to initiate contact or risk him thinking I was asking for too much too soon. However, the stark truth was that time was running out for Dad and if John wanted to meet his grandfather – as he had said he would like to – it had to happen soon. Like immediately. With my heart in my mouth, I put my fears aside and called him, outlining the urgency of the situation.

To my huge relief, John didn't hesitate. He said that he would be in Bath the next morning.

That Sunday meeting between John and his grandfather turned out to be a bigger family reunion than I had planned.

As soon as she heard that Dad's life was likely measured in days rather than weeks, of course my sister Christine also wanted to be at his bedside. I understood that Christine wanted to be as involved in Dad's care as she could be, but at the same time I wasn't sure I was ready to involve her in my reunion journey. Not yet. When Christine announced that she was on her way to the hospital, I panicked. I explained what was going on and asked her to try to avoid the time when John was likely to be there.

Of course, fate had other plans and Christine and her family arrived just as John did. What could I do except introduce John to everyone at once and hope that he didn't think I'd planned an ambush? Fortunately, he didn't seem to be at all upset or surprised to find that he would be meeting the whole family at once. My sister was delighted to have the chance to meet her nephew, whom she hadn't seen since his baptism when, dressed in her school uniform, she had cradled him in her arms for a few brief minutes.

Those pictures from the baptism seemed especially poignant as I watched John reacquainting himself with his aunt and his grandfather and meeting the cousins he hadn't known existed until a few weeks earlier. I felt so proud of him, as he navigated the situation with ease. Though the circumstances of the meeting around a hospital bed were not ideal, it was still a special moment.

Chapter Thirty-Nine

To all our surprise, John's arrival that day seemed to have a miraculous effect on Dad's condition. Though he was still determined that he would be refusing treatment, in the hours that followed, Dad came out of what had been deemed irreversible kidney failure to the extent that he was moved out of his side room and back onto the general ward. Feeling very much better, the next day Dad had a memorable exchange with the consultant who had outlined his prognosis in such unkind terms. As he approached with his team of underlings in tow, my father in a firm and strong voice made his position clear: 'Get out of my sight. I never want to see you again.' I wish I had been there!

Meeting his long-lost grandson had given Dad a new lease of life. He was enchanted by John and they soon established a relationship of their own. Dad gave John a pen that he had saved for many years, perhaps in the secret hope that one day they might meet. They connected over their shared interest in history. Dad was proud that his grandson had turned out to be a high-flying scientist with a doctorate. Dad's belief in the importance of higher education was still strong.

It was wonderful to see John and Dad talking so happily together, but painful too. During one of John's visits, we took Dad back to the cottage so that John could see our family home. Settled in the sitting room, Dad turned and looked at me.

'Look how wonderfully things have turned out. Look at what a great job they have done. You must be so grateful to his parents who have raised him to be such a fine young man.'

Those words went straight to my soul causing as much pain as any bullet or sword. More so, for some reason, because of where we were. I don't know why Dad felt the need to say such a hurtful thing. Now a lot of what he said is true and I take my hat off to John's parents – they did do a great job – but what riled me was the implication that they did a much better job than I would have been able to do had John not been adopted. That is what I was supposed to be grateful for? I am sure Dad's intentions were good; I sincerely believe that he was never aware of how what he was saying might be received by me.

And perhaps Dad said those things to defend his own heart. Maybe it was because meeting John had shown Dad exactly what had been taken from him, too. When I lost the right to be John's mother, Dad lost the right to be a loving and involved grandfather to such an exceptional young man. Perhaps unable to deal with the fact that he had not tried hard enough to offer me any other choice but to relinquish John for adoption, the only way Dad could cope with his own grief for the years we'd lost was to tell himself – and me – that John would not have thrived in my care.

It was hard for me to forgive Dad for those careless words, but I knew I had to try to let them roll off me. Dad was grieving his own loss and when the moment came, I wanted John to be able to remember him fondly. I sat in the chair across the sitting room from them both and stayed silent.

When Mum was in the last few weeks of her life, she said at one point something about being so angry when I was pregnant and also how upset she was at the things Tim's father had said. That was the whole depth and extent of our conversation, slightly closed off by me as all I said in reply was 'it was OK'. How sad that we missed the opportunity to share what we thought and felt in more depth. All I will say is that when I said it was ok, I really meant it – by then I had really resolved and accepted the things that had taken place between me and Mum. That was not the case with Dad.

It wasn't fair on him really, as I do believe that it was Mum who behaved in the harshest way towards me. Yet somehow I was able to simply accept Mum for who she was and all I feel is sadness about her not being alive today.

Dad did not have an easy time with me before he died. We did talk a bit more though. He told me that he had really wanted my son to come home and to be brought up by Mum, but that Mum refused to do this. In many ways he put the blame for the harshness I experienced within our family on my mother. I don't think it was a question of him wanting to absolve himself. I think it was likely a fairly accurate portrayal of how things were. However, my internal response was to think – well, what stopped you from standing up for me? What stopped you from fighting my corner more determinedly? What stopped you putting your foot down and telling Mum that my baby was going to come home, that this was non-negotiable?

Yet it must have been a terrible dilemma for Dad. At a logical level, I recognise that, as well as being stuck in the middle between his wife and daughter, he would have been under so much pressure to conform to the social norms of that time. No-one he turned to in a position of authority gave him even a hint of other options or an indication that support might be out there. Every single person he spoke to reaffirmed to him the need for secrecy to protect his family's reputation and told him that 'the plan' in place was the best way forward for all concerned. In reality, all of these factors came together at such great expense to me. This made me feel very angry and disappointed – and it was my father who, unfairly, bore the brunt of this.

I just can't understand what stopped me feeling the same sense of forgiveness towards Dad back then as I had done towards my mum. Overall, I think I grew up in an environment where there was little room to be forgiving or forgiven and I was as harsh on my father as my mother had been on me. I am also really harsh on myself, somehow feeling that I still deserve to be punished. Only now the person dishing out the punishment is me – therein lies a little circle of complexity.

It may also be because what Dad thought of me and how he articulated this had affected me so greatly. Somehow it was easier to deal with the cold shoulder approach, which is what I got from Mum in the early days when I was back at home.

During the last few weeks of Dad's life, we muddled through. Although there were times when he said things that really got to me, as already described, he could also hit the nail on the head. Towards the end, we were back in his house talking through all the things I would need to do after his death when all of a sudden he turned to me.

'Everything you've achieved in your life, you've done by yourself,' he said.

That spoke volumes to me as an acknowledgment that he and my mother had not always supported me in the ways that I needed.

Somehow, in turn, it opened up the channel for me to acknowledge everything positive that my parents had given me – including the values, principles and beliefs that I still live by today.

Chapter Forty

As spring came around, life began to settle down a little. Stephen's cancer surgery had been a success and he was back home. Dad had spent a week at a local hospice for respite care and everyone was optimistic. Dad wasn't fit enough to live alone, so we'd come up with an arrangement whereby he was given a place in a seven-bedded care home close enough to his house so that when he felt well enough, he could go back there during the day, returning to the home for an evening meal and to sleep. I was still having to drive many hundreds of miles a week, but at least there wasn't the same sense of urgency. Stephen's doctors were confident that he would continue to get better and Dad's condition seemed to have stabilised.

One day in March, I got up early and drove to Bath to spend the whole day with my father. It was a good day. We talked happily about life and about John, of course. Dad was the very proudest of grandfathers. At 7.30 in the evening, we decided it was time for Dad to get some rest. I left that evening so happy that everything between my dad and I was just how it should be. Things were back to being relaxed between us, with both of us really enjoying our precious day together. As I got up to leave. I leaned in to kiss him on his forehead and I started to walk away, giving him a little wave and blowing him another kiss. He smiled and reached out offering to give me a hug. I went back. Little did I know just how precious that hug would be.

The following morning I received a call.

'I don't know how to tell you this Michelle, but your father died in the early hours this morning. I'm so sorry.'

The owner of the home explained that she had checked in on my father and found him awake. She had sat with him for a while before leaving to make him a cup of tea. When she left, my father was enjoying the blackbirds leading a magical dawn chorus. When she returned, he had passed away.

Dad told me he wanted his funeral to take place at the local village church, despite it being C of E. Dad had never given up his Catholic faith but since retiring from the RAF, he had become very involved in the local community and the parish council. The church he chose might not have been Catholic, but I knew that it was one that meant a great deal to him.

I was greatly moved and pleased when John told me that he wanted to be at the funeral to say 'goodbye' to the grandfather he had known for such a short time. His decision reassured me that I'd been right to call John to Dad's bedside at the hospital. At the same time, John was sensitive to the secrecy that had surrounded my pregnancy and I'm sure, was himself still processing everything that had happened in the last few weeks. He arrived without fanfare and sat quietly at the back of the church.

Dad's was a good funeral, spoiled only by the presence of two people, who had always liked to think they were better than our family. Throughout the time I'd known them, they were constantly fishing to find out what had really happened when I was away from home in the winter of 1971/72. At Dad's funeral they commented, 'We would have expected to see a few more people here,' though I would have loved to say, 'quality is better than quantity, and I would have preferred two fewer.' I kept my cool and comforted myself with the thought that they had no idea they were missing out on the gossip they'd been after for so many years. My son had been sitting right behind them in the church and they hadn't the faintest clue.

John came back to the house after the ceremony and mingled with the rest of the mourners. I was so glad to have him there. Looking across the room and seeing him, with his face that looked so much like Dad's, was a big comfort to me. There was a beautiful symmetry in the moment too. Dad had been there for John's baptism, his first religious rite of passage. John was there for Dad's last. How wonderful it was that they'd had the chance to get to know one another.

Chapter Forty-One

Later that same year came the most surprising twist of fate.

Though Stephen and I had come together at a time when many of our friends were having children, we had remained a unit of two. Secondary infertility – not having another child – is common amongst women like me, who gave up a child for adoption, for psychological and physical reasons. In my case I'd just always felt that having another child would be disloyal to Baby Tim. I had also thoroughly absorbed the strong messages from St Anne's Mother and Baby Home, from my parents and from the welfare officers at the adoption agency that I was a bad girl. I was not fit to be a mother and I would be incapable of raising a child successfully.

My experience had left me with a double helping of shame: first for having got pregnant outside marriage, then for being the sort of woman who gives her baby up. What kind of mother was that? For his part, Stephen was happy not to have children, enjoying the freedom it gave him and us to pursue our own interests. So even though Stephen and I knew that we were together for the long haul, we didn't ever try for a baby. At the same time, as we got older we weren't always particularly careful about *not* getting pregnant.

We found out in a supermarket car park. My period was late and I'd been feeling a little odd. At first I put it down to my age. I knew the perimenopause could affect the menstrual cycle and I was around the right age. It didn't seem possible that I was pregnant but all the same I threw a pregnancy test into our trolley as we did the weekly shop.

Once I'd bought the test, I found I couldn't wait to get home before I used it. I ripped the test open in the ladies' loo, peed on the stick and carefully carried it out to the car park where Stephen was waiting for me to tell him the result.

When the blue line appeared a few moments later, I stared at it in astonishment. I turned to Stephen, who was staring at the line in astonishment too.

We were having a baby.

Never in a million years had I expected that pregnancy test to be positive. Such a whirlwind of thoughts went through my mind as the possibility sank in. It was as though I had been thrown back in time and was my 16-year-old self again. My first instinct was to tell myself that the test must be wrong. Denial, my old friend. But two further tests taken back at home delivered the same result.

It was a delicate moment. So indoctrinated had I been by my parents and the nuns at St Anne's, that I found myself automatically reacting to the news with fear. All the feelings I'd felt first time round bubbled up and it was as though I was waiting to be told that I'd disgraced myself again. I was going to be in so much trouble, my inner 16-year-old warned...

Fortunately, I had Stephen beside me. We've always been a real team. He pulled us together now by reassuring me it was good news and that we could do this together.

Over the next few weeks, as the baby grew inside me, so did my confidence. I was scared but I was also increasingly excited. Perhaps I could do this after all.

I reminded myself over and over that I hadn't given John up for adoption because of any lack of love or care on my part. I'd given him up because there had seemed to be no other option. In 1972 I was a teenager without the means to support myself and a baby. I'd been told so many times that he would have a better life without me. Now I was a grown adult and I was married to a man who was my rock and who would be beside me no matter how difficult things might get. The situation could not have been more different. Finally, being in reunion with John seemed to have given me permission to imagine an alternative future, one in which I got my chance to be a mother to another child.

Tentatively, I began to look forward to a moment when I would hold a baby in my arms once more.

In a strange echo of my first pregnancy, I was determined to keep this surprising second pregnancy to myself for as long as I could, not wanting to tempt fate but also wanting to savour the early changes in my body that had been too frightening to consider when I was a teenager. This time, I didn't attribute any tiredness or nausea to stress. I was pregnant and I was going to enjoy every minute of it.

Secretly I prayed for a girl, thinking that to have another son would be harder. I thought John would find it easier to have a little sister too I thought that I would find it easier to raise a girl, having not been able to raise my boy. If my second child was a daughter it would mean that John could keep his unique place in my heart. My son would always be my only son.

I started to get excited about the prospect of having another child. Even though it was early days, I started to ponder on what it was going to be like and all the things I needed to prepare over the next few months.

One day Stephen and I invited our elderly neighbours over for tea. Marjorie and Dorothy were retired teachers and lifelong friends. Sadly Dorothy had dementia and was already very frail. At the end of our jolly afternoon, they prepared to go back next door, Dorothy found she was unable to get back out of the big comfy chair into which she'd sunk. I wanted to help her but as I got up to walk across the room I felt a strange cramping sensation and had to ask Stephen to go over to her instead.

Stephen and I waved Marjorie and Dorothy off. Shortly afterwards, I went to the bathroom and discovered that I was spotting. It isn't unusual to pass a little blood in the early stages of pregnancy so I tried not to worry. However, it wasn't long before I was losing more blood than seemed right. I phoned the local GP's surgery and spoke to a female GP who I didn't know that well. She told me that I should go straight to the hospital in Basingstoke and tell them she had sent me. At my age – the wrong side of forty-five – my pregnancy was already considered high risk. 'Yours is a very precious pregnancy,' the doctor had said.

Stephen drove as quickly as he could but I think I knew before we got to the hospital that we were on a hopeless mission. The bright lights of the accident and emergency department offered no comfort, not when I felt with my heart that my baby was already gone. A hurried scan confirmed the bad news. There was no foetal heartbeat to be found.

Having told me the worst, the doctor overseeing my treatment decided that I should be taken upstairs for a 'D and C', a dilation and curettage to clear any remnants of the pregnancy from my uterus. Feeling battered enough already, I refused, telling the medical staff that I wanted to let nature take its course.

Chapter Forty-One

'It's over,' I said. I just wanted to get back home.

After such a terrible night, I probably should have taken a few days off but of course I didn't. Stephen, for whom the loss must have been every bit as difficult, did all that he could to protect me in the fragile days after I came back from hospital without our child. As it happened, I was booked to deliver a training course for a big corporate client the day after I miscarried. When Stephen couldn't persuade me to cancel the course altogether, he insisted on driving me to the venue and back each day, spending three hours on the road each morning and evening to make sure I didn't have to make the journey alone. I was determined that the course would go ahead as planned. No-one needed to know what I'd been through and I don't think anybody could have guessed. Throughout my life, I'd often found that I did some of my best work under the worst possible circumstances. I'm good at digging deep to gather together emotional resources which are also so well-tuned to handling tragedy and loss.

I was also of the belief that so close to the miscarriage I might actually benefit from taking some 'mental space' to allow the unconscious processes of grief to begin. For most people, the idea of 'mental space' conjures time away from the office, some peace and quiet, but I took the view that if I filled the front of my brain with work, the back of my mind could be left alone to do its heavy lifting. That was my reasoning and a strategy that I know helps me deal with whatever comes my way.

I was glad though that Stephen came to fetch me. The November weather was terrible, with howling winds and lashing rain. It seemed to reflect how we felt inside. We didn't talk about what had happened. I needed to be in my own space, Stephen too. Talking about the miscarriage wouldn't bring our baby back after all.

Much as I wanted to, I couldn't avoid doctors altogether. In the aftermath of the miscarriage, the GP who had sent me to the hospital called me in to see her. As we talked, she metaphorically wrapped her arms around me with her compassionate take on the situation. She empathised with my decision not to have a D and C, telling me that she would have refused the procedure too. I was glad not to receive a lecture.

Her previous words on how precious this pregnancy had been echoed in my heart. She didn't have to tell me that it was unlikely it would happen again. I was heading towards 46. Doctors refer to pregnancies as 'geriatric' when the mother-to-be is over thirty-five! We both of us knew that it had been my last chance. But it was good to feel validated by the GP's understanding. She understood the enormity of it all even if I still wouldn't fully allow myself to feel it.

Thankfully, because the miscarriage happened at nine weeks, Stephen and I had yet to tell our most of our friends and families. John and Liz didn't know. Neither did my sister. Apparently, I told Linda and Maria, not that I can remember. Linda says I only mentioned it briefly and in such a low-key way she began to wonder if she had dreamt it.

At the time of the miscarriage, I was still processing the fact that I was pregnant. After the miscarriage, I continued to process the loss in my own way. I didn't grieve outwardly. I'm not sure I have ever allowed myself to grieve inwardly either. Whenever I think about it, there is just emptiness.

Chapter Forty-Two

Though there can be no closer bond than that between mother and child, when reunited after such a long separation, you really do not know each other at all. My son had been missing from my life for 28 years.

As I spent time with him in those early days, the gaps in our knowledge of each other showed themselves all the time. The first meal I cooked for him is a case in point. I knew that John was very much into healthy food so I made a selection of salads including one with the superfood of the moment, which was quinoa, thinking John would really enjoy this. John ate the quinoa and declared it delicious but I later discovered that it gave him tummy trouble. As it did me. Both of us had just eaten a meal that neither of us could digest well and we both gave the impression to the other it was lovely!

It felt ridiculous to have to ask questions of my own son as though he was a stranger.

'Do you take milk in your tea? What about sugar..?'

Just like with the quinoa, was he just being polite when he accepted other foods I put in front of him? I really had no idea what he liked in any area of his life.

In the early days of our reunion, I'd read all that I could about the subject – all the books on the various lists held at places like NORCAP and the Post Adoption Centre, plus whatever research papers I could find on the Net. None of them did it for me, though. On the story front, there were just too many stories that sounded like fairy tales compared to my own experience. Mothers and their children were reunited and suddenly all was well in their respective lives. They felt an instant connection and the child had a sense that this was his or her mum. There was also talk of an initial honeymoon period with lots of excitement and the wonder of it all. I read about mothers and children meeting up frequently and having lots of contact, especially in the first year, via phone calls and emails or letters. None of this matched what I was experiencing and to a large extent reading this stuff just made things worse for me. I was not meeting the norm.

I was hesitant to call or otherwise make contact unless invited to do so. I was nervous about interrupting my son's life and causing any challenges between him and his adoptive parents, his mum and dad. I didn't want to upset them either. I knew they'd gone into the adoption in good faith. I was scared to overstep the mark or assume too much. I had no idea what place he felt I had in his life. We were both constantly putting our best selves forward, only wanting to share how things were good. We were both so polite to each other – ours was nothing like a relationship in a family. We both wanted to make our reunion a success and we were on our best behaviour at all times.

As the years went by, we found we had many things in common. There were strange coincidences too. John's father Tim had been a keen diver. John also liked to dive. Tim was good at writing, while I was very definitely more science than literary minded, but John also enjoyed writing and perfectly combined Tim's natural skills set with mine. The matches that were hard to explain, other than by nature, went even further. When a good friend of mine watched John give a talk, he was astonished by how similar John's mannerisms were to mine. John hadn't grown up watching me and Tim but we were there in everything from the way he walked to the way he talked.

It was a beautiful journey of discovery together, like we were exploring uncharted territory. We found we approach problem-solving in the same way; we like to share our thoughts out loud with the listener acting as a sounding board. It's never the finished product at that stage.

We have both married people who are the opposite to ourselves. Stephen and Liz are people of few words. When they have something to say it is a considered comment or statement. John and I both talk a lot! It's perfect; Stephen and Liz sit quietly, maybe both reading a book and occasionally exchanging amused expressions as they watch John and I chatting away at nineteen to the dozen! Somehow we've ended up similar in nature and married to people who are similar too. It is wonderful and amazing that, despite the passage of time and our complete separation for so long, there is so much that we share.

Chapter Forty-Three

After reunion I found I needed the support of people who understood my story more than ever. I had tried all sorts of counselling over the years but nothing ever seemed to make the difference I hoped for. In fact, I'd found that in some ways talking about my teenage pregnancy and Baby Tim's birth was retraumatising.

I joined The Natural Parents Network (NPN). I disliked the name, 'natural parents' implies that there are 'unnatural parents' too which I think is disrespectful to adoptive parents. This seems like a good place to say I dislike the term 'birth-mother' even more. To me it epitomises how I was treated, like a machine and not a person. I call myself John's first mother. It implies another and I hope gives respect to both. With the NPN, I was keen to connect with other first mothers who could help me to make sense of what I was feeling.

I also made contact with the Post Adoption Centre. The PAC supports people on all three sides of the adoption triangle, but to me, it did seem a little light on support for first families. Just once a year, we were invited to come together at the PAC's offices in London. I very much looked forward to those days. We would take food to share, light candles in memory of everything we'd lost, and talk through our experiences. However there was something about those days that seemed to amplify my feelings of low self-esteem. Even the facilitators − first parents themselves − seemed to worry about asking for too much. I felt that collectively we were akin to impoverished first cousins needing to be grateful for even this one meeting a year.

Once, after not hearing from John for several weeks, I found myself struggling with getting the right balance between my hopes for our relationship and what was reasonable to expect. I knew that above all else I had to respect John's need for space but living with the silence and the uncertainty and the not knowing where things were between us was unbearable.

I decided to call the Natural Parents' Network advice line, which was staffed by other first-mothers. I was sure I would find a sympathetic listener at the end of the phone, someone who had been through the same stage in reunion and could tell me definitively how to handle the situation for the best. The volunteers were not formally trained but there to provide support and assistance as best they could. Hats off to every one of them. It must have taken great strength to manage your own emotions while listening to each caller's story.

However, to my disappointment, the woman who picked up the phone did not initially make me feel better at all. When I told her about my struggles to handle the long periods of silence, her response was not empowering in the least. Instead, she echoed the feelings of low self-worth which had been plaguing me ever since I found out I was pregnant all those years ago. Her key message to me was not to raise my expectations and essentially be happy with any 'crumbs' that fell from the table. She all but said, 'Be grateful for whatever you get. This is all we first mothers deserve.'

I'd been trained as a coach and I could easily recognise the self-defeating patterns in her behaviour. It wasn't long into the call before the roles were reversed and I was the one listening to the woman I'd asked for advice, with a strong sense that she should give herself a break. Like me, she'd been a young woman when she gave birth, practically a child. The odds had been stacked against her. She didn't think she had a choice.

Hearing her story sparked such a strong reaction in me – a fierce sense of us as mothers deserving so much more than this. I found myself thinking that come what may, from now on I was going to set myself higher expectations. I felt so sad for this person who was 'helping' me. No matter how low an opinion I had of myself at times, hearing another person with such low hopes brought out a sense of injustice and my fighting spirit. In the end the call really did help me, though perhaps not in the way that the person on the other end of the phone might have expected.

Chapter Forty-Four

As I grew more confident in my relationship with John, I became more comfortable with telling people about having had a baby so very young, the adoption, and that he was back in my life. My closest friends already knew and were universally happy for me. Reunion was a rocky road at times, certainly not a linear one and I needed my friends more than ever. Even so it was still hard to let them see just how difficult I was finding it at times.

While John and I were separated Mother's Day had always been particularly hard. I was a mother yet I had no idea where my child was or even if he was still alive. After reunion what would this annual day of celebration mean? How would it manifest itself? John now had two mothers in his life, but I knew he only had one mum and that wasn't me. Was it reasonable for me to have any expectation of acknowledgement on this annual event?

For the first Mother's Day after reunion, April 2nd, John sent me a card. This came out of the blue. I had not expected it. Although it did not mention 'Mother's Day' on the front or inside it conveyed a sense of warmth about us having been reunited. My heart soared and it meant so much to me. But the next year and the year after my heart sank as those Mother's Days passed unmarked. Although I knew it was totally unreasonable to have any expectations, that lack of acknowledgment left me feeling we had taken a backward step.

At a rational level, it was understandable. John had much to process. He was on his own rollercoaster ride. I'm sure his initial agreement to our contact was primarily curiosity but as we started to build a relationship, it became confusing. I'm not sure he had anticipated the emotions it would unleash for him or the complexities which were coming to the forefront. With no shared life experiences and both of us still unable to talk freely because of our fear of upsetting the other there was no way of us knowing exactly where the other person was, or what we needed or expected.

When John and I first started writing to each other back in 1999, his relationship with Liz was fairly new, but it soon became clear that they were serious about each other. John introduced me to Liz early on. We met at John's house and we quickly formed a bond. Liz has always been (and still is) an amazingly supportive person, both to John and to me as one of John's mothers. However, Liz was also thrust into the centre of the secrecy. Liz was unable to tell her own parents about me or that John was seeing me, just in case something slipped out when her parents and her potential in-laws were together. Despite this, Liz was great at helping John and I move forward.

I don't remember exactly how it happened, but one day, while we were all sitting in the kitchen of the house she shared with John, she managed to create space for me to be bold enough to talk a little about where I was coming from. In the course of that conversation, I dared to mention that some kind of acknowledge-ment of me as one of John's mothers would be amazing. Well, every year since I have always been sent a Mother's Day card.

Although back then it was still hard having to remain a secret, the cards and phone calls meant a great deal to me.

I was delighted when in 2007, Liz and John told me that they had decided to get married. Unfortunately, that good news was to be tinged with pain for me. Though by now seven years had passed since that winter's afternoon at Jane Austen's House, John still hadn't told his parents about me. This left them both with a huge dilemma. John and Liz both wanted me to be at the wedding, but it was going to be impossible to have me there while John still hadn't found the right moment to break the news of our reunion to his mum and dad. They didn't want to have to lie about who I was.

'Then tell them!' I wanted to shout. But of course, I had to be respectful of the boundaries John continued to place between me and the rest of his life. From the very beginning of our reunion, I had been clear that John's feelings and needs came first. As the child who had been given up, he had to be at the centre of everything that happened now and things had to happen at whatever pace was right for him. I understood his reasons for not feeling able to be open about our ongoing relationship. He had great love and respect for his adoptive family and was still terribly worried that they might see his being in contact with me as some kind of betrayal. He was sure they would be hurt to find out that he wanted me in his life when they had given him so much and had always been there for him.

In an attempt to make up for my being unable to attend the wedding, John and Liz were careful to involve me in their preparations and reassure me that even though I couldn't be at the ceremony in person, I would be very much there in their hearts on the day. I tried to let that be enough and made sure never to even hint that it might not be.

Julia, one of my best friends, who has two sons of her own, was a fierce champion in the reunion process, always ready to come to my aid when things felt especially hard. As the big day approached, Julia suggested that while I couldn't be part of the wedding party, there was no reason why I shouldn't be at the church for the ceremony itself. She'd come with me. It was a nice idea. Perhaps we could slip in late and leave early? But John and Liz were getting married on a remote Scottish island. I could hardly claim to be 'just driving by'. Everyone on the island that day would be an invited guest. A stranger would definitely stand out. We even, jokingly, explored whether I could watch from the mainland with a pair of long-range binoculars – this part of the conversation was about adding a little humour as a strategy for coping.

Ultimately, on the day that John and Liz married, all I could do was stay home and hope that they had a wonderful time. I was delighted they were getting married, but it was a day when I cried a lot!

After the wedding, John and Liz invited me to visit to show me the photographs. They were careful not to remind me too much of what I had missed, focussing on pictures of the two of them as a newly married couple, rather than showing me pictures of their guests. When they did show me a photograph that contained Liz's parents and John's adoptive family, they were careful to refer to everyone by their first names rather than their 'titles' of mum and dad. It was a very sensitive thing to do.

I understood why I'd had to stay away and I was grateful to be included in the planning and to be first on the list to see the photos, but ultimately, it reminded me of what I still didn't have. The shame and secrecy that had surrounded John's birth still whirled around us like fog. Would we ever be able to escape it?

I was so fed up having to be kept a secret. Secrecy was defining me as someone who lived in a glass-fronted cupboard.

I could be taken out at times but then needed to be returned. Most of the time the glass was opaque. Inside my cupboard I knew what was happening outside but I couldn't be seen. I was connected but disconnected.

There were so many secrets. John needed to make sure everyone had their own little box and I had my cupboard. I did my damnedest to make sure that John never saw that asking me to stay hidden was emotionally challenging, but seven years on it was increasingly hard. Not just because I wanted to shout from the rooftops but because I could see that John too was trapped by not wanting to hurt or appear ungrateful to the people who had brought him up. Every time he talked about his 'Mum and Dad' in front of me, the conflict was there in his eyes.

Just as I had spent years striving to make up for what I'd done by being the perfect student and businesswoman so that I could be 'acceptable' to my family again, I think John, as an adoptee, had faced a life-long struggle to feel worthy of the family that had adopted him. Like many adoptees, he had grown up with the idea that he should be 'grateful' for their love, that he was 'lucky' to have been taken in, without ever considering the weight of the happiness he had brought to his adoptive family in return.

Like me, John had become an inveterate people-pleaser, putting the well-being and wishes of everyone else before himself. Even when that was to his detriment. I could tell that keeping me secret was not easy for him at all.

I made sure that John never saw when things were bothering me. I would work hard to keep every emotion contained until he and Liz had left my house or I was on my way home from theirs. After leaving their house, I often sat on the roadside letting all the emotion out until I was able to be confident I was in a fit state to drive home, which was an hour away. I never felt it was appropriate for me to burden my child with my issues. They were mine to deal with, not his. As his mother I needed to be there to support him, not the other way round.

Chapter Forty-Five

After all these years in reunion, John and I still continued to be on our best behaviour with each other. While it was a lovely indication that we both wanted our reunion to succeed, we also needed to build some shared history together and create our own memories. Two specific things come to mind, the first being Monty.

After getting married, John and Liz decided they wanted a dog. Having had a Jack Russell Terrier growing up, Liz was delighted when I told her there was a litter needing homes in my village. The three of us went to take a look. The owners proudly showed us the pups and talked about when they would be ready to leave. We were all having a wonderful time, making a fuss of the puppies, when a comment stopped me in my tracks.

'It's hard enough for us to part with these puppies, I can't understand how some women can just give their babies away,' one of the owners said.

I remember the awkward moment of silence that descended (at least it was awkward to me). They had no idea who John was or of our history. I don't know if the comment registered with John but it was an awful moment for me. The couple were not people I felt a rapport with when we arrived, but this comment reinforced the level of judgement I felt was still out there towards people like me. It reminded me of the dreadful couple at my father's funeral.

The moment passed. A few weeks later Monty was happily ensconced in John and Liz's house. He was a cute little puppy and very intelligent. It wasn't long before he was calling the shots – which he still tries to do to this day. He has a special place in my heart as he has become woven into the fabric of John and I starting to build our own shared memories and experiences.

At one point I felt really brave. I asked John and Liz if they wanted to go away with us for a short holiday. I had long since recognised that we were 'oh so polite' to each other, never wanting to put a foot wrong. I was hoping that by being away for a few days and sharing our love of walking, we would both be able to relax and just be ourselves. I also knew that it would be emotionally hard so when they said 'yes', I booked two lovely cottages at a farm on the South Hams coast.

We are long-standing customers at the farm and we know the area well. We took John and Liz on all our favourite walks and took turns to cook in the evenings. Our separate cottages were there for us to return to whenever we needed some personal space. It was wonderful! The sun shone, we walked, we talked and we laughed. I really felt we were building happy memories of our own. After John and Liz returned they made a wonderful video from their photos and I still love watching this today, treasuring the memory of this time.

Although I was still a secret within John's family, I started to share that I had a son a little more widely. This was huge to me. With my immediate neighbours who are great friends and like family to me, everything went well. It was lovely to have them meet him and for him to be so welcomed. Outside this little circle I was much more cautious.

I started by introducing John to two local friends in my village. I had explained to them how delicate it was, and what an early stage we were at; that although I am his mother, his mum was his other mother, for all the reasons I have written about earlier. I could have got up and forcibly removed one of them from the room when she repeatedly called me John's mum and went on and on about how lovely that we had found each other!

Thankfully, John took it in his stride. I did not. Although I know she was well intentioned I was very disappointed that my wishes were not respected. And it made me question whether it was the right time for me to introduce John to people in my life, except for my very closest friends, whom I knew I could trust in every way.

Chapter Forty-Six

Back in 2005 I took one of those tests that measures your stress levels according to what's been going on in your life. As I counted up the major life events I'd ticked off even since 1999, I started to realise just how much I had been up against.

I'd endured the loss of both Mum and Dad in quick succession, the worry of Stephen's cancer, the uncertainty of my reunion with John, getting a new business off the ground and a miscarriage. Not to mention the continual energy expenditure involved in managing my fears and phobias, especially with travel, and keeping them under wraps from all but a few. Added to this were all the years I'd had to pretend I'd never had a child, never able to acknowledge his existence or grieve for my loss. The amount of stress I had been dealing with was off the scale! And all the time I just kept trying to push it down as it bubbled up. I'd only taken three days off in the past 12 months.

By 2010 it was very clear my coping mechanisms were not working for me. Although I had curtailed the travel, not only was I still working ridiculous hours, I'd been soothing myself with food and the weight was piling on. I drank two glasses of wine every night. That might not sound like a lot but it was more than my body could cope with. My weight reached 89kg, which given that I am not a very tall woman, meant that I was into the obese category.

Ironically, while I'd been eating addictively, I had been following a three-year course in nutrition. Thanks to my consultancy background, when I completed the course I was able to start lecturing in the nutrition field. As well as working with my corporate clients I became a visiting lecturer at the college where I had qualified. Alongside my nutrition qualifications I had also completed a significant amount of training in communication, namely coaching, consultancy and facilitation skills.

At the college I taught second- and third-year students clinical consultation skills. It must have seemed strange to my students to have me teaching them when I was a walking, talking example of the challenges of putting nutritional theory into practice. I may have graduated from the same course with distinction, but I was really struggling to 'walk the talk'. However my lectures were extremely well received and I had great rapport with the students. Somehow I think they saw past my 89kg to my passion for the subject.

It's very easy to tell someone who's struggling to keep their weight under control to 'eat less', but as I myself demonstrated, it's never that simple. 'Eat less' didn't begin to address the emotional complexities behind my obesity.

It seems obvious now that I had been eating to 'stuff down' painful feelings, and drinking to escape from any that rose to the surface. Other things were at play too. My body was complaining at how hard I had been pushing myself. A routine blood test revealed that my thyroid function was extremely low, despite, in my opinion, no obvious symptoms. When the test results came back, I was given an appointment with the doctor who had been so kind to me in the aftermath of my miscarriage.

She told me she was 'gobsmacked' by the results, which seemed so improbable that she ordered another test. She was sure the numbers must be a mistake as I appeared so well, but a second test confirmed that they weren't.

Given that I had spent the past 30 years living on pure adrenaline and cortisol, it's no surprise that something finally had to give!

I knew I had to try something different. Even before I got the shocking thyroid result, I had realised this and had already started to take steps in the right direction – literal steps to begin with. Carrying so much extra weight, I struggled to walk up a hill, but I was determined to undertake the then fashionable steps programme at 10,000 steps a day. I also decided that all those empty calories would have to go.

Though I would not say that I was addicted to alcohol, I was definitely drinking too much. I didn't like feeling out of control but there was a part of me that was drinking to numb my emotions. Fortunately, I had long since moved on from the vodka and pineapple juice that I used to drink in Germany. I only ever drank good quality organic red wine. Giving it up was difficult as it had become an evening ritual, but once I made up my mind that was it; zero units a week ever since. I'm not sure I've continued to conquer food quite so well, especially while writing this book – chocolate! But, back then, without the familiar crutches of food and drink, I had to face my situation head on.

Even before my thyroid issue was diagnosed, I had lost two stone, contributing to the scepticism with the first test result. After the thyroid result was confirmed by my GP she said, 'it's an insidious disease and you won't know how unwell you were until you feel better'. She was right. As my thyroid function improved, many other things improved too.

Chapter Forty-Six

Perhaps it was getting a grip on my physical health that helped me to take the next step, to seek to heal my mental health and understand everything that had happened since the day I discovered I was pregnant with John. I knew that I still needed to do more to change the way my life was panning out.

I needed to go right back to the beginning.

Chapter Forty-Seven

My story was so jumbled up in my head: a maelstrom of memory loss and distortions which at times I have found to be unsettling. Unfortunately, as it unfolded it only got worse.

For almost all of my life since my son was adopted, I had thought the following was true: I looked after John at the mother and baby home for six weeks until one morning it was time for me to leave without him. I went home, went back to school and somehow put my life back together.

This is what I told anyone with whom I shared this part of my life and this is what I believed to be the absolute truth.

In 2012 I decided to speak directly to the adoption agency to learn more about my past. There are lots of reasons for wanting to do this, but what is important is the outcome. Luckily Carole, the social worker who had helped with my reunion was still working at the adoption agency and she explained that I could come over to the office and look through an edited version of my file. I decided to take the train to Bristol as soon as I could.

I assumed that the day would be an easy one. After all, as far as I was concerned, I already knew most of the facts! The city of Bristol and the journey there was, thankfully, familiar to me, and Carole would pick me up from the station. Still nothing could have prepared me for what I was to discover.

In the office, Carole handed me a thin blue folder, upon which was the title Timothy Peter Pearson. I opened it eagerly. To begin with the report confirmed the things I knew for certain, like my son's date of birth and weight. But after that it was like reading someone else's file.

To start with, there were several factual errors, talking about me being one of four children and describing my boyfriend as an apprentice. Tim was one of four and it was his brother who was the apprentice, not him. Not a good start, especially as elsewhere in the file there were various forms, which we will come back to, filled out by Tim and myself that clearly showed accurate information.

However, these aspects were insignificant by comparison to what I read next. In neat black typing, another document talked about me being very attached to my baby, and Tim and I having a series of meetings with my assigned social worker at St Anne's and back home at my parents' house. The conflict in my heart was evident, leading up to the final meeting where Tim and I confirmed our agreement to adoption as the best way forward for all three of us.

What I read gave me no comfort. Instead it unleashed the full force of my own self-hatred. I had been weak, I had not fought hard enough. Why had I not taken the tiger by its tail and stood my ground? Although it clearly stated that my parents would not have allowed me back home with my son, why had I not tested this by just refusing to step away from my child? I had failed.

After this upset, I was physically and mentally in no fit state to travel, but I had to get home. Carole dropped me off at the station. I was still clutching my copy of the report. Somehow I made it onto the train but I felt so spaced out and once again everything was surreal.

The journey back to Basingstoke, where Stephen was due to pick me up, might have ended in disaster were it not for a couple of drunks, who decided to sit in the seats across the table, right in front of me. They were amiable drunks, who seemed determined to spread their happiness to me and to others in the carriage. As they larked about, sharing their jokes and engaging me in their rather incoherent conversations, their comical antics went a long way towards helping me. They made me laugh and be present, sharing in their fun. By the time I got to Reading where I had to change, I felt grounded again and I left the train with a smile.

Chapter Forty-Eight

Back home, reality as I perceived it came back in. I was inconsolable. The factual errors in my file were also on my mind. I kept reading and re-reading the summary file and each time I found something else that fuelled my growing anger. The file said that Tim had 'shared his pocket money' with me. What? That made no sense at all, especially compounded with the mix up with his brother's details. Tim was at school, but he worked in a garage. He had shared his *wages* with me.

I rang Carole and the summary file was duly corrected but it made me think that I had to see my original file. I had to see first-hand what had been written there about me, not rely on a document that contained so many inaccuracies. What did the original file say? Did it contain the same mistakes or had these occurred when the summary was prepared?

'That is not possible' was the initial reply to my request to see my original file. In an instant I took that tiger by its tail. There was no way on this earth that I was not going to see it. Recognising my steely determination, Carole looked for a compromise. Apparently, no other mother in my situation had ever asked the agency to see their file. Once again, I was a trailblazer.

Emails and phone calls were exchanged. The proposed compromise was that I would go to the offices, as before, and someone would read the file out loud to me. I could not believe what I was hearing. I held my ground and eventually Carole agreed it might be possible for me to see my file, as long as she sat next to me throughout. My email reply made my position unequivocal:

26th April 2012

Just to be clear on my expectations / understanding: I am expecting to be able to read through my file myself, albeit with you alongside me, rather than having it read out loud to me. If I find that I need to have some time alone (on the day) to process what I find (e.g. wanting to re-read something alone), I would like you to respect that too.

I do understand that you and your manager have my welfare in mind but here is some feedback for you to give to your manager:

a) The suggested approach of having my file read out to me made me feel that I was being treated like a toddler rather than an adult. I felt blocked, insulted and angry – yet again people trying to determine what's best for me – I'm glad we've moved on from that to our current plan – please continue to treat me as an adult capable of making my own decisions and being responsible for my own actions and outcomes.

b) As I'm sure you're aware, reading / seeing stuff on a page has a totally different effect on the brain compared to hearing something being read out – the former is what I need to do. I quite understand that there will be information that could trigger strong emotions but I'm prepared for that and indeed welcome it. Sometimes to move forward one has to read / deal with any bad stuff that might be in a file too!

c) Part of the healing process is simply understanding things as they are/were - not having things dressed up in any way. What information there is and any interpretation of things in the notes is a reflection of a very different society etc. I handle things much better if I believe that I'm getting a full account, upfront and open. The previous summary of my file, while helpful in some ways, was never going to be enough for me – it always begged the questions – What might be being hidden from me? / What else might there be in the file that may be helpful to me?

d) No-one other than me really knows what helps / hinders – No-one can filter information, even with my welfare in mind, and know that they have given me all that will be helpful. Please let me get on with my healing process in my own way. Seeing what's there, and indeed what's not there, also meets the upfront and open aspects that are important to me.

One of the most troublesome aspects of my current situation for me is my complete loss of memory. This includes the period from after giving birth through to well over a year or more afterwards. It's like my identity has been stolen. While I understand the protective nature of amnesia, filling in the blanks from whatever information is still in existence is helpful. If going forward blanks remain, somehow that is easier to accept as a protective effect – at least I've given putting the jigsaw together my best shot...

...Whatever is in my file is what is there – I think your support on the day will be helpful in processing things but I reiterate that I need to do things my way. Instinctively I know what I need to do to heal and I am very determined! I've also had quite enough in my life of people thinking they know what's best

for me, as I'm sure you understand…

A period of silence followed, after which a date was agreed.

I knew I had to be better prepared for the second meeting. I certainly would not be going into it blithely assuming there could be no more nasty surprises. I'd been lucky, having those amiable drunks to distract me on the train back from the first meeting. This time, I took no risks, arranging to stay with my dear friend Maria in Bath rather than try to travel back to Hampshire alone.

I knew that Maria would know how to comfort me, if that was what I needed. She had been such a good friend to me and my family over the years. We had already been through a lot together. She had been like a guardian angel to me, and to my mother when she was ill. Working as a nurse on nights in the hospital, whenever my mum was there, Maria would make sure to visit her at the end of each shift, reporting back to me on how well (or not) she was being cared for. I always felt safe in her care.

One major issue still remained. One condition. Although I could see my original file, I was told that one particular sentence would be redacted. What on earth could be so bad I wondered? Always taking things upon myself, I decided it could only mean that I was a worse person that I had imagined. What had I done that was so bad that it had to remain hidden from me? Biding my time, I held back from responding immediately. I needed to have that file in my hand, but I was not going to accept this condition.

Chapter Forty-Nine

The big day dawned. Once again I met Carole at the station and she drove me to the agency offices. We'd already had several interim chats over the phone so she knew exactly how I felt about the redaction. Equally she was clear on the need for the agency to be able to keep back any information they felt could be harmful to me. During the drive I managed to glean a little more – the redacted sentence was considered to be so derogatory and judgemental, she was worried it could put the agency at risk of being sued. That made me laugh. It had never been about something I had done in the past – the agency staff were concerned about what I would do *now*.

I was so curious to see what had been written about me back in 1971/72. What could be so bad that it could not see the light of day in 2012? I was even more determined that this redaction was going to be removed.

With the papers finally in front of me, my heart was beating fast. Together, Carole and I began to take a look at what was there. The first thing that surprised me was the date of the first entry. According to my records, though I had been at the mother and baby home since the middle of November, I did not have my first meeting with social services until the middle of December. The entry recorded:

> *Michelle is at St Anne's and the fees are being met by social security payments supplemented by her parents at £3 per week. Wilts LA was prepared to pay the fees only if she went to Devises apparently.*

Already, in those first few lines it was evident to me that what was *not* said was going be as important as what was. I suspect my parents chose to pay a contribution to ensure that I was far enough away from our family home to avoid embarrassment. I had brought such shame on the family, I must not be seen by anyone who knew us. I needed to be kept out of sight. That made sense, as I do have a memory of my parents paying some of the costs, not from the time itself but, from Dad having cited their payment as evidence of support, on one of the occasions we attempted to talk about things before he died. I was supposed to be grateful.

Following on from this were all the inaccuracies I had pointed out in the summary file. It was interesting to see the carelessness in these notes when the correct data had been given to social services by both Tim and I, as evidenced in the same file by the forms we ourselves had completed with our details. It did not inspire confidence.

By now my attention had already been drawn to the rest of what was on the page. I could already see the tape below covering up part of the text. That redacted sentence. Before I got to it, there was more I had to read. I could see that before I gave birth I said that I wanted *the* baby to be adopted. However, after having *my* baby, things changed for me. I suspect that the idea of adoption had been easier for me to consider before I gave birth. After giving birth, I was a mum and life was not so simple.

Chapter Forty-Nine

The social worker wrote: *26th Jan:*

Met with Michelle and Tim. Tim wants to be a child welfare officer which will require 5 years further study after he leaves school this summer. This would not be possible if they kept the baby. Michelle also wants to continue at school and feels they are both too young to settle down and support a child. However Michelle feels that she cannot make up her mind definitely until she is away from Chepstow and without the baby – she would like the baby fostered for a few weeks before she decides finally. She said she cannot take him home. I said I would have to ask Fr. Hall.

The redaction, shown as **XXXX** below, came in the next sentence.

The social worker had added:

'*I spoke to Sr. Dolores afterwards. She said Michelle is very attached to the baby.* XXXXXXXXXXXXXX'

The more I looked, the more distressed I felt.

What lay under the tape?

What was there that I was not allowed to see?

One might think it would be easy to remove the masking style tape, but 40-year-old paper is fragile and the text started to come away. I'm not sure I can convey fully the effect this had on me – it was *me* that was tearing. I was being pulled apart. Part of *me* was being destroyed.

I may have been angry and upset about the blanking out but now this anger was enhanced exponentially. I tell you what, it is lucky that in the end I managed to read the words by holding the torn paper against the window up to the light. I'm not sure what would have happened if that had not been possible or if I had been left in any doubt about the actual wording in the file. Interestingly, Carole had not stopped me when I moved to uncover the redaction. Seeing my distress, she actually came to my aid at the window as we traced over the writing that was revealed, backwards of course from our view.

So what was all this fuss about? What on earth could Sister Delores have said that was considered too awful to show me 40 years later? Especially coming as it did after a comment on how attached I was to my baby.

I think it's best if I write out the two sentences, the one deemed so terrible and the one before, just how they are in the file. I want to do this because it's the juxtaposition of two themes in the sentences that says a lot to me.

'I spoke to Sister Delores afterwards. She said Michelle is very attached to the baby. She also feels that Michelle has a low moral standard.'

There it is. First, notice the 'the' in front of the word 'baby'. Important I suppose for the staff to keep a sense that my baby was not mine. It was *the* baby, *a* baby ready for dispatch to another family. Meanwhile, to me the redacted part conveys a sense of 'Michelle is very attached to her baby but we need to remember that she is unfit to be a proper mother'.

And, just for completeness in terms of adding judgement and supposition the notes then say:

'Sister Delores thinks that Tim is very realistic, I feel, myself, that Michelle thinks she will lose too much freedom by keeping the baby.'

Hang on a minute, I thought. Where did all of this come from? I'd just finished talking about my uncertainty about proceeding with adoption and wanting time to think things through away from the home and away from my baby – basically to see if I could actually go through with the adoption given how bonded I already was to my baby two weeks after giving birth.

Tim may well have been realistic given our ages, lack of parental support, us being still at school with no financial means, but these comments reflect the general impression I got across the whole file – I was a bad girl, Tim was a good boy.

I read on, until I came to the 14th February, on which day the social worker added a note to the file saying that she had spoken to Sister Dolores, who told her that Baby Tim was ready to be taken away.

My Baby Tim and I were parted.

Chapter Fifty

The files filled in a lot of gaps. Tim and I continued to have meetings with the social worker after I left St Anne's and went back home to Bath. In a note from March, when the social worker came to visit me and Tim at my parents' house, she writes:

'They would like to keep the baby and wondered if he could be fostered for 18 months. I suggested that this was not good child care and the baby would suffer. They agreed with this and we discussed the various means of how they could keep the baby. Michelle's parents are not prepared to have the baby at home. I suggested that Fr Hall could ask the Parish priest to advertise in his weekly bulletin for accommodation for Michelle and the baby until Timothy finished his A levels.

'Timothy appears very sensible and asked for 2 weeks to think about the possibilities. If they decide to keep the baby he will leave school, otherwise they will have him adopted.

'I sensed that Timothy was not very well accepted by Michelle's family. Neither Michelle nor Timothy asked how the baby was or if they could visit.

'I arranged to see them again in two weeks when they hope to have a decision.'

Away from Chepstow, I must have been missing my baby terribly and I had asked the social worker for more time. I requested that we look into the possibility of a fostering arrangement that would allow Tim to finish his A-levels, while we kept in close contact with our baby with a view to being reunited as a family as soon as we could be.

Here it gets a little hazy again, in that the files don't match what would have been true. Tim was due to sit his A levels in June, only a few months away. Why was 18 months being referenced for fostering, but accommodation for Baby Tim and I for the much shorter period?

The notes above also raise the expectation of the social worker coming back to me with news on possible accommodation but there was no follow up on this at all. I wasn't even told how my baby was or that I could visit him. Wouldn't it have been up to the social worker to suggest that? She knew the rules. I didn't. Why wasn't she more pro-active? The files showed unequivocally that I had been looking for ways to keep my baby. Of course I wanted to see him!

A little later, on the 16th March, a month after I left St Anne's, it seemed the decision of adoption as the way forward had been made. I was defeated. The social worker met with me and Tim again:

'They appeared to have talked it over in great detail and have come to this decision. I explained the procedure of adoption.

'Michelle did not appear to be very emotional but Tim was very quiet throughout the interview.'

To me, the last sentence implies that not appearing to be emotional was a sign of my bad character, and that Tim being quiet showed his good character. There was no concept of me being shell-shocked and frozen having made the hardest decision of my life.

The note ended:

'Michelle says her parents do not really want the baby to go for adoption but they do not seem to be making any effort to help Michelle to keep him. I said we would go and place the baby out for adoption as soon as possible.'

Chapter Fifty-One

There was a definite theme to the records I was shown by the adoption agency. Tim good, Michelle bad. Tim was the sensible one. I was the one with pie in the sky ideas about how we could raise Baby Tim ourselves.

Before social workers were called social workers, they were called 'moral welfare officers'. The change of title only came in the late 1960s and it seems to me that the social worker looking after me, Tim and Baby Tim had not brought her views in line with the new branding.

The file also contained a copy of a letter that I was sent in April 1972, shortly after Baby Tim was placed with his adoptive family. To this day, I am amazed by its style and tone. The social worker wrote:

'You will be pleased to know that baby is progressing well and the adopters are very fond of him.

'I enclose a form which you must sign before a magistrate, who should endorse the enclosed birth certificate. If you have any difficulty in finding a magistrate, I am sure the local police will help, but in any case if you are in difficulty would you please get

*in touch with me. I should be most pleased if you could let me have
the forms back as soon as possible.'*

I think this letter really demonstrates the complete lack
of support and the degree to which my feelings, emotional
state and situation were ignored or misunderstood. The letter
contains not one question asking after me, or anything advising
me where I could go for support if I was struggling in any way.
And what a statement to make that the adopters 'are very fond
of him'. It sounds like they are talking about a cat not a child!

Before I left the adoption agency offices in Bristol that day in
2012, I asked for a moment to look at my file notes alone. To my
astonishment and relief, I was granted that opportunity. The
minute Carole was out of the room, I took out my phone and
started photographing the pages in front of me. I didn't know
then whether I would be given a copy to keep and I worried that
this would be my one and only chance to read them. I had spent
the years since 1972 believing one version of the past. I had
discovered that the truth was quite different. I was not leaving
without a full copy of that file in my possession.

It is still unsettling not to have a single memory of anything I
saw described in the complete file. Every meeting, conversation
and event has been completely erased from my conscious mind.

To their credit the agency forwarded me a copy of the file
at a later date, but as I left that day with those photos, I felt as
though I was carrying pieces of myself back home.

Chapter Fifty-Two

The effects of this second session at the agency were massive. For all these years I had been living under the mistaken belief that I had firmly decided to have my son adopted before I left the mother and baby home and that I had stayed there for six weeks, which matched what I had read somewhere as standard practice.

My emotions were all over the place. I hated myself for making the decision to have my son adopted; seeing it there in black and white brought it home with such a punch. I was proud of myself for being as feisty as I had been, exploring ways to keep us together, but I was disappointed in how I had failed. I was angry at how I was being portrayed as a bad girl, someone with 'low moral standard' compared to Tim who was seen as the good guy, the realistic one, the sensible one.

All of this was bad enough but the most shocking discovery from my file was yet to come. A decade later, in 2022, my feelings have turned to anger. To unpack this we need to go back to my file notes dated 26th Jan 1972, repeat and extend the earlier quote to include the next few lines.

'...Michelle feels that she cannot make up her mind definitely until she is away from Chepstow and without the baby – she would like the baby fostered for a few weeks before she decides finally.

'She filled in the forms. I gave her a medical form, which can be completed on Tuesday next. She will also get a birth cert.'

'She filled in the forms', such an innocuous sentence and one that had escaped my attention until recently, when I asked myself 'what exactly were those forms?'

On that day, 50 years ago, I had been a mother for less than a fortnight. I'd been out of hospital for just a couple of days. I must have still been tired and confused; my hormones still unsettled. I don't see how anyone could have thought that I could possibly be in a fit state to make a serious, life-changing decision. Yet that is exactly what I was being asked to do.

I signed two forms that day in January 1972. The first was a 'certificate of acknowledgement' showing that I had read and understood 'Adoption of Children – an explanatory memorandum'. The second, more important form, was entitled 'The Adoption Agencies Regulations 1959 – Fourth Schedule'. This document consisted of 17 questions. Question 13 was *'If the mother is alive does she consent to the adoption?'*

I had answered YES to this question.

Question 14 asked the same of Tim and for his consent. He had also answered YES. Our signatures are side by side at the bottom of the form.

We had both been asked to sign this particular form on the very day the file says that I was not sure what I wanted to do. There is nothing in the file about anyone taking time to explain exactly what we were signing. Although nothing was irrevocable at that stage, why not wait until I had the time and space I was asking for? Surely anyone within two weeks of giving birth is still all over the place; never mind the stressful and pressured circumstances here. It seems like shockingly bad practice. Talk about hidden agendas. I feel manipulated. I'm sure Tim does too. All these subtle pressures and nudges to keep us on the conveyor leading to the single outcome of adoption make me very angry now.

Having seen my files, I definitely didn't feel any better. So much of what I had thought was true had been shown itself not to be so. I had ventured out to find out everything that had happened since the day I discovered I was pregnant with my baby Tim, now my son John. The volume of new information, there in black and white but still totally outside my conscious awareness was such a shock.

I have so little memory. Like Alice beginning her adventures in Wonderland when she finds the rabbit hole under the hedge, I was finding my world an unpredictable place full of riddles. I was also filled with a sense of curiosity. How could my mind just wipe out all those memories? Why had I done this to myself? What else didn't I know and not even know I didn't know? Who am I when most of my memories remain outside of me, existing as events only revealed to me in photographs or on paper?

I had been to the Post Adoption Centre on several occasions for the annual first mother meetings. Although the direct support was very limited, I noticed that Dr Liz Hall, a clinical psychologist with several decades of experience of working with patients presenting with complex trauma including related amnesia, was scheduled to give a talk open to all. I made sure I was there.

Listening to Dr Hall, suddenly everything that I was experiencing made sense. She explained that faced with something that elicits fear, when past the point of fight or flight, animals freeze. Once the threat is over, they physically shake to release its effects. Humans hold on to our trauma because we truncate that process. We may not have conscious memories but they are still there, held outside our awareness physiologically, as well as psychologically. It's for that reason that we sometimes overreact for reasons we can't articulate. This was something I had often wondered about. Why did I find it so hard to go to new and unfamiliar places? Why can it be so anxiety provoking to be by myself, especially at night? Why had I reacted so strongly when being moved off a project at work that I had nurtured? Why do I find myself moved to tears on some days when seemingly nothing has happened to cause such an outpouring of emotion?

I was so impressed by Dr Hall's talk that I approached her afterwards to find out if she would be willing to work with me on a one-to-one basis. It was a turning point for me when she said 'yes'. We worked together over a number of months and in 2014 she gave me a formal diagnosis of post-traumatic stress disorder: PTSD.

Dr Hall's care made a significant difference to me. She helped me to understand why everything I was experiencing was very normal after what I had been through. Dr Hall also helped me to process and release some of the trauma via Sensorimotor Psychotherapy. It's an interesting process, which involved asking me questions to be answered in my head. As a physiological response set in, rather than try to stop it happening, she would direct me how to work with it via movement or postural changes, or by verbalising my inner experiences. It was a bit like learning to ride a wave, staying on the surf until all its force is dissipated and spent.

This was such a different approach. At first it was hard to stay away from 'telling my story', the approach that at times

I had found made things much worse for me. Now I also understood why with some counsellors (not all), it had only served to re-traumatise me. I cannot speak for anyone else but Sensorimotor Psychotherapy was the right fit for me and my work with Dr Liz Hall made a lasting difference.

Sadly Dr Hall passed away in 2020, which is such a big loss to so many people in addition to her own family and friends. The positive change in me after working with her was transformative. I owe her a great deal of gratitude and I am pleased to be a small part of her great legacy.

Chapter Fifty-Three

By 2015, John and I had come on a long way but most of my closest friends, despite knowing a great deal about him, had still not met him. It was coming up to my 60th birthday and I was planning a party: 60 people for a sit-down meal in my garden. I begged and borrowed tables, chairs, gazebos, outside lights, everything that I needed. A local village caterer made a selection of salads and these were served with a very large cold joint and vegetarian options. A group of friends made the puddings. Everyone who was important to me was going to be there, including a few blasts from the past who I had not seen for a very long time. I invited John and Liz, of course, and they said 'yes'. Wow!! This surprised me but it was so wonderful for me. I was going to be celebrating my 60th birthday with my closest friends, my husband and my son…

One thing I was sure of was the meal had to have a seating plan. I felt it would be daunting for anyone, let alone John & Liz, to step into a large group of people most of whom they had never met. I chose to seat John and Liz with my oldest friends. Maria and her husband Chris, Linda, Julia and Peter did a splendid job of looking after them both.

What no-one knew was that Liz was pregnant. She and John had only recently shared the exciting news with me and I had kept it to myself. I later discovered that during the course of the evening, Liz told the whole table that she and John were expecting. It was a very special moment at the party for me, showing as it did how comfortable Liz and John were in the company of my dear friends.

Another poignant moment came later that same evening. Maria's husband Chris, whom I have known since I was 16 (post the adoption), is a singer and guitar player. When he first started seeing Maria, he used to gig at a coffee bar called the Four Square, which was affiliated to the church. For my birthday, he had written a song especially for me and at an appropriate moment, he sang and played it to the party. It was beautiful, not only as a song but for the care and thought he had put into it. At the end of the song, John went to talk to Chris and thanked him for what he had done. This took how I was feeling to a whole new level and I know it meant a great deal to Chris too.

Everything about the evening was perfect. It was lovely to be with all my friends, including those I have not mentioned specifically here. The weather was perfect. It was a beautiful warm and sultry night. The food was delicious. The wine and conversation flowed. The very next day the heavens opened with stair-rod rain. I had been blessed on my 60th, the most special birthday in my life.

Chapter Fifty-Four

Understandably, John and Liz were quite nervous about becoming parents. At the same time, I was absolutely terrified about becoming a grandmother. When I look back at those photographs of John's christening at St Anne's, I see a young woman who had everything it took to be a mother. I look so happy and relaxed as I hold my baby in my arms. There is such joy in my face. I was everything a mother and a mum needs to be. When John and I were parted, my belief in myself as a mother went with him. I had not trusted myself to even try for another child until John and I were in reunion and that dream had been cut short too.

I wanted so much to be a good grandmother to John and Liz's baby but I was fearful. I worried how I would feel holding a new-born in my arms. How would I cope in a grandmother role with zero experience of ever having raised a child? The abandonment and rejection I had experienced and the narrative that I was unfit to be a mother were all etched into my identity. Did that mean I'd be an unfit grandmother too?

As the birth approached, Liz and John seemed to be taking a very laid-back approach to getting ready for their baby's arrival. They didn't have a pram. They hadn't prepared the nursery. 'We'll get round to that,' they told me. I sometimes wonder if they had gone into a mini version of my type of denial in order not to become overwhelmed.

Because Liz was an older mum-to-be, she had been told that she would need a managed birth. She knew she would be given a specific date to go into hospital and planned accordingly.

I did not expect to be involved until much later on. Though John and I had been in reunion for 17 years by this point, he still hadn't been able to tell his parents that I was back in his life. It simply never seemed to be the right time – most recently, because his adoptive mother had been in ill health. For this reason, I expected to be among the last to know when my grandchild was born and to have to wait until all the other grandparents had visited before I had a chance to meet him or her. But fate was about to step in.

Liz's planned admission date was brought forward. Unfortunately, this meant that Liz's parents, who were living overseas, would not be able to get to the UK in time. They had booked their flights according to the original admission date.

At the same time, John's adoptive mother's illness meant that his parents would not be able to travel up to support them either. It was sad news for John and Liz but brilliant news for me. John asked me if I could come and stay at their house to hold the fort while the two of them were at the hospital.

I was delighted to help. I busied myself with looking after Monty, buying a few items I thought would make life easier for Liz, and cooking a couple of home-cooked meals that would save them the hassle of having to shop when they came home with their baby. I wanted to relieve them of the boring day-to-day jobs so they could concentrate 100% on their new life as a family of three.

It was wonderful to be able to do everything a proper 'mum' would do for her son and his wife, though of course I was still painfully aware that it was only possible because John's adoptive mother was so unwell and that Liz's mother was still having challenges getting back to the UK. All the same I decided to make the most of being able to share this precious time. However, as I waited to hear that the baby had arrived, I worried how I would react when I first met my grandchild. Would it bring difficult emotions to the surface?

John and Liz had not asked to know the sex of their baby. I worried about that surprise. What if their baby was a boy? How would I feel if seeing John's son brought back the unhappy memories of us parting, suppressed for so long, in one painful rush? Or what if it released the memories that I would love to have back – my own first few weeks as a mother, being a real mum to my son, taking care of him – those precious memories, which cruelly had never surfaced so far? What if everything flooded back and I couldn't cope or found everything intertwined in some kind of surreal way? I needed to be strong for them. I needed the focus to be on them and their new-born, not on me.

Eventually, I got the news.

'It's a girl!'

Later that day, I went over to the hospital and John and Liz, so tired but proud, introduced me to their lovely daughter, my granddaughter. When they placed her in my arms, I held her carefully like the precious treasure she was. Peering into her beautiful face, I felt an instant burst of love and warmth. All my fears melted away; I was present in that very moment with such happy tears welling up inside me.

When John and Liz came home, they asked me to stay. There was almost a pleading look in their eyes as they did so. I suspect their own nervousness as first-time parents coming home with this precious bundle in their arms had kicked in. But I knew they needed this time alone. They needed to find their own way. It was time for me to go back to my own home. I also sensed it was time for me to be alone. While I had coped with everything, this was an immense moment in my life too and I needed space to allow my thoughts to go wherever they needed to go.

It was fantastic that I had been able to be there for John and Liz and that I saw my grandchild as a new-born but, as to be expected, the first few weeks were filled with family time for them. Liz's parents came to stay. Then John and Liz took their daughter to meet John's mum and dad.

I stepped back into the background.

Chapter Fifty-Five

Over the next few months things settled down as John and Liz got into a normal new parent routine. They were wonderful at encouraging me to come over to visit and to spend time with my granddaughter. I felt part of her life and very connected. It seemed just like a blink in time before she was sitting up, crawling and taking her first tentative steps. Being able to share these moments came with mixed emotions for me – delight for what was happening right now and an increased sense of sadness on what I had missed with John. On several occasions after I left their house I found myself struggling to remain on an even keel. As ever this was out of sight of anyone else.

My granddaughter's first birthday showed me just how complicated things were too. If there were going be family celebrations, there would need to be two separate sets, including one where I was on my own with them. I was fine with this, but mention it here to highlight how difficult it must have been for John, still working so hard to keep the different aspects of his life in their little compartments while trying to please everyone involved – including me.

In our celebration we introduced my granddaughter to her first taste of chocolate. I recall how much she disliked it then but, like so many things, that has changed!

One thing that never went away was my lack of confidence that I would be able to look after my granddaughter by myself. It is fair to say I don't do babies – I go to great lengths to avoid them whenever I can. They stir too much up for me. Although it had been different the moment I held my granddaughter in my arms, no matter how hard I tried I could not shake off my sense of not being capable. These days things are a little better but only just. Even when she was old enough for her pre-reception class, I was still finding it difficult to handle where I was at.

On one occasion I had agreed to stay over to help out. Liz and John were both heading off to early morning meetings. All I had to do was keep an eye on my granddaughter from 6am, get her up, sort out breakfast and get her over to the school by 8:45. For me this was like undertaking surgery without having qualified as a doctor. I was so scared that something would go wrong, that something dreadful would happen and it would be all my fault.

Even after I had dropped her off at school, I was still in catastrophising mode. I had cut a plastic tag off an item of clothing and I could not find it. What if it was trapped in her clothing? What if she found it and tried to eat it? I was straight back in the car and over to the school insisting that we checked. Nothing was found. I can only imagine what the schoolteachers and classroom assistants thought of me. After being reassured that they would keep an eye out, I left totally exhausted. I had completed my responsibilities for the day but my own lack of confidence and belief of being incapable stayed with me for much longer – indeed it is still with me today.

* * *

With the arrival of their daughter and indeed during the pregnancy, John and Liz had started thinking about what to do with the secrecy surrounding me. After all, at some time in the future their child would start to talk and most likely the cat would be let out of the bag. It was especially difficult as John and I had already been seeing each other for so many years. The edges of the compartments John had kept everyone in were beginning to fray.

Not ready to talk to his parents, John turned to his two sisters Jo and Jane – both older than him. They were delighted to hear of his reunion with me but also recognised the challenges John faced in telling their parents, in getting the tone and the timing right. I'm glad John had great support from both his sisters, at last he had two other people close to him that he could talk to. From the outset John wanted me to meet his sisters, his nieces, and Jo's husband. This desire was reciprocated by both Jo and Jane. It was a little challenging with Jane as she lives in New Zealand. Definitely outside my travel range!

Things were about to get a whole lot more complicated with these five other family members being drawn into the secrecy.

John is very close to his sisters. He is younger than them by quite some years and thus his relationship with Jo, his oldest sister, in particular was almost maternal. She'd often looked after him while their parents had to work. As I found out later, Jo was the one who had given him relationship counselling the first time he had a girlfriend, including teaching him the importance of treating his partner with respect. Thus it was a defining moment in my relationship with John when the day came for me to meet Jo for the first time.

I was almost as nervous meeting Jo as I had been the first time I met John. I felt my anxiety rising as I drove to John's house. Was it really the best time to meet her? What would she think of me? What if she didn't like me? How would that affect my relationship with John? It was a day of great importance. As I approached the house I said to myself, 'I don't know if I can do this.'

But the moment I saw Jo, I knew it was going to be absolutely fine. She stood in the doorway and we walked towards each other once I was out of the car. We wrapped our arms around each other and she gently stroked my back as if to soothe me, rather like a mother would do to her child.

'How lovely to meet you. I have been looking forward to this so much,' she immediately said.

She made reference to me as John's mother and that acknowledgement had me fighting back the tears. My emotions ran so deep and evidently the same was true for her.

Because Jo was 10 years John's senior, she and I were actually pretty close in age. In subsequent conversations I learnt that she could relate to me very easily, having seen a classmate get pregnant when she was about the same age as I had been. Jo had seen how kindly that girl was treated, with full support from the headteacher. Thus, Jo knew how different things might have been for me if I'd had similar support.

On the day we met she'd brought lots of photographs from John's childhood to show me and within minutes, we were chatting away like old friends. You couldn't shut the two of us up. The conversation was completely natural. It says something about how easily Jo and I got on, that John and Liz soon left us to it and drifted upstairs to their respective home offices to take the opportunity to get some work done.

As we parted that day, Jo told me that if I ever found myself near her home, I should make sure to drop in. A few months later, I went to the Bristol Balloon Fest with my nephew. We were travelling up from Devon and the day before I rang Jo to tell her we would be nearby. I thought that perhaps she'd think it was a bit short notice. On the contrary, Jo said she was delighted to hear from me and invited me and my nephew to breakfast before we set off to the event.

Jo cooked us a feast with just about everything one could possibly think of having on the table for the first meal of the day. I guess that, like me with John, she had no idea what I could or could not eat, but without doubt there would be plenty. Both Dan and I felt so welcome. Meeting Jo's husband was great too. Dan, he and I share a passion for photography and before long they were absorbed fully in their conversation leaving me and Jo to pick up where we had left off. Talking with Jo recently, she revealed that meeting my nephew that day was a shock to her in a good way. There standing in front of her was someone who looked just like her brother.

We made all sorts of plans that day to meet up again but as ever fate had other ideas and would take us in different directions for a little while longer. The health of her mum, John's mum, was heading into serious decline. Jo became the prime carer, stretching herself thin between her own home and the home where she had grown up with John and Jane. This, and later the restrictions with Covid, meant it would be several years before we were able to see each other again. In the meantime, I did meet her daughters, both equally welcoming and delighted I was back in John's life. Now, I look forward to the day when I will meet Jane in person – something we both want to happen. While Skype has connected us well, I want to hug her like Jo and thank her for all her support to John.

I suppose it isn't surprising that the connections, especially with Jo, were immediate and deep when we had something so big in common: the fact that we all love John and want the very best for him.

* * *

Sadly, John's mother and I never met, as she died in 2017. By then she had discovered that John and I were seeing each other. I don't know how this came to light, but ironically her immediate response was to say to John, 'Don't tell your dad.'

Yet more secrets!

Chapter Fifty-Six

John's mother's death was a time of great sadness for everyone in the family, especially for John's dad. At first, he wanted to stay in their family home but with his own health failing it became harder for him to manage, despite excellent care and support from John, Jane and especially Jo.

In 2018, he moved to be closer to the family, into a bungalow just a few doors away from John and Liz. This was fantastic for John. It took the pressure off his sister Jo, and gave him the opportunity to enjoy a period of father-son richness similar to the time I had spent with my mum before she died.

At the same time it was difficult for me. I'd got used to being able to visit John and Liz at home and spend time with my granddaughter. It felt like I had to go back and live in my opaque glass-fronted cupboard again.

John and Liz could not risk me being at the house, just in case John's dad popped round for a cup of tea. I could not be involved in school activities for fear of the teachers mentioning me when John's dad was taken to an event. John struggled with the secrecy and was committed to telling his dad, yet every time he decided he was ready, something would happen to derail the plan. John also knew the clock was ticking on the possibility of his daughter chatting away about me in front of his dad too.

As for me, I was back on that rollercoaster. I had got to like how our relationship had developed. I had got to the stage where I was comfortable picking up the phone and even asking if it was ok for me to come round. Now I needed to step back again. I needed to accept that we could only meet up away from John and Liz's home, maybe for a picnic or just a walk. I was already so tired of being a secret and now things were heading deeper into that territory again.

By then, I had spent over 45 years of my life with so much of my identity non- existent. Now the little seeds of me being a grandmother were unable to flourish. At a rational level I understood fully. At an emotional level I was distraught. Once again I was in a situation where I could not speak out. The last thing I wanted to do was to make life any more difficult for John. I was in total agreement that things had to be done properly. I wanted John's dad to be told but only when the time was right and I could see so clearly why that time never came. I knew I had to suck it up and carry on. I had to keep whatever I was feeling about my own situation to myself. At least this time round I had Stephen and my very dear friends to support me.

I got by. John's father had the most amazing care and I hope that since he has died John is comforted by knowing what a great job he did. I only wish I had met him and had the opportunity to get to know him. From what I know, he was an amazing man and John was lucky to have him in his life.

I hope John and Liz had no idea how bad it was for me. I took genuine delight in hearing about John with his dad and seeing, albeit if not first hand, what a great job John was doing. I knew from my own experiences how important this time was and how much it would mean to John after his father died. That in itself helped me enormously and in the same situation again, I would want it to be just as it was. As I've said before, my issues are my issues. Like any mother I am here to support and love my child and put him at the centre of the universe.

Chapter Fifty-Seven

While on my own journey, it is sometimes hard for me to get my head around the staggering fact that in the UK during the 50s, 60s and 70s there were up to half a million of us 'bad girls'; young women who found themselves in similar situations to me. Although every story is unique, the similarities in terms of the challenges I faced with parents, the Church and the agencies involved are pervasive and frightening.

In 2010 a group of mothers like me formed an action group called Movement for Adoption Apology, or MAA as it is known. The aim of the group is acknowledgement for the injustices experienced by first-mothers in the 50s, 60s and 70s. In the early days, the focus was on a Government apology.

The members of the MAA have worked tirelessly for several years, never giving up on their mission for the injustices we all faced to be acknowledged. Towards the end of 2021, the group's voice was finally heard and the UK government opened an inquiry into forced adoption, chaired by Labour MP Harriet Harman. The enquiry is entitled: The Right To Family Life: Adoption of Children Of Unmarried Women 1949 – 1976. Its remit is to 'examine whether adoption processes respected the human rights, as we understand them now, of the mothers and children who experienced them, as well as the lasting consequences on their lives.'

Birth (first) parents, adoptees and adoption professionals were invited to give evidence. At the time of writing (March 2022), the process is still ongoing. Reading through the written evidence, once again I find the stories presented by the first parents are very familiar indeed.

Among the many expert advisers giving evidence at the enquiry was Dr Michael Lambert, a sociologist at Lancaster University, who spoke about social policies and the role of the welfare state in adoption practices during the decades under investigation. I wrote to Dr Lambert, to ask him to clarify the position regarding financial support for single mothers in the 1970s. I wanted to find out if any resources had been in place that might have helped me to raise my baby on my own? I told Dr Lambert the circumstances. That I had been just 16 years old, still at school with nowhere to live if I didn't go back home, and no-one supporting me in any way. Could state support have enabled me to manage on my own? He wrote back.

Hi Michelle,

It is good to hear that you are publishing a book based on your experiences as these can so easily be lost to current and future generations without taking the time to put them 'on the record'...
I am also sorry on a personal level that you have suffered the experiences you have at the hands of the state and from officials who are nominally supposed to help you.

At a very practical level I will reply to your question 'could state support have enabled me to manage on my own?'.
Possibly. I hope you have a sense from my evidence and my

background research that lots of mothers did, in fact, keep their children. Not all were forcibly adopted. So in theory this could have happened. However, context is important. Most of the different types of officials did all they could to prevent this from happening because adoption was the 'solution' in their view. Both removing a child from a single mother to 'better' parents and a proper family, combined with the single mother then starting her own 'proper' family later. Keeping a child was a negotiated affair and not easily done because it often meant cutting yourself off from family, friends, and even putting yourself further at the mercy of the same officials who were trying to remove the child.

At a social policy level it was hard. In 1972 there was no legal right to housing. This only came in 1977. Before then you would have been at the mercy of the local authority points system which weighed 'need' (i.e. the circumstances in which people lived and their claims on housing such as living in slums) against 'respectability' (i.e. accumulating points over years by being on the waiting list). Although decisions were often made by officials, in smaller rural authorities these were made by members of the council which gave plenty of room for personal decisions to creep in. It was not democratic...

...Paper entitlements were often meaningless in how they were judged by officials at the time, and there was an enormous amount of ambiguity and discretion built into welfare systems which gave considerable scope for stigma and moral judgements to creep in or – more often – take centre stage....

With thanks and best wishes,
Michael

So there you have it. That last paragraph sums it up for me. I was at the mercy of the moral judgements of others.

Was I even informed of all of the options available to me back in 1972? There is no record anywhere in my file of anyone ever talking me through financial support, no matter how meagre. How could I make a truly informed choice when vital information was missing? Why didn't anyone tell me what might have been possible? Why didn't anyone come to my aid to help me navigate through the system?

When the Movement for Adoption Apology was first formed. I was invited to join the committee, but I declined. Back then, I was still of the opinion that I was solely responsible for my son's adoption and I needed to be held to account. I was the one that needed to apologise. I needed to apologise to my son. I had been weak. I had not fought hard enough to keep him.

Even recently, when I first saw the cover of the book you are holding in your hand, with the title 'Taken' written large above my name, my mind raced straight to this default position, one I had held for the past 50 years. 'My son wasn't "taken". I gave him away. I was an unfit mother.' Even if I had no memory of doing so, I had signed the paperwork.

Today, 50 years later, my journey of discovery has shown me there was only ever going to be one outcome, no matter what I did. Everyone around me was going to make sure of it. Now I am angry. An apology alone from a politician will never do it for me. I want people to understand what happened to me and other women like me. I want justice, which includes acknowledgment and pragmatic actions to support mothers who, like me, are still tormented by what happened to them. I am so pleased the Enquiry is underway and I am very grateful to the MAA for working so hard on behalf of all of us.

Chapter Fifty-Eight

Sometimes it is hard to get your head around how bad it was for women like me, given how different social mores are now. In the United Kingdom, becoming pregnant outside marriage no longer carries the stigma that tore me and Baby Tim apart. These days, around 40% of children in the UK are born out of wedlock. Being the child of an unmarried mother hardly raises an eyebrow any more. Indeed, many women choose to become mothers without involving a 'father' at all, turning to donor conception instead.

That said, despite the change in attitudes, with babies no longer taken from mums simply for them being unmarried, life in the UK is still tough. Many families and not just single parents are struggling to put food on the table and to pay the bills. Perhaps because being a mum was denied to me, I am in awe and admiration of mums and dads, especially single parents, who are doing an amazing job bringing up their children in difficult economic times.

I am also deeply saddened when I see mothers who, despite all their best efforts, find themselves facing adoption orders today. I'm not talking about situations where children need to be removed from harm. I'm talking about the parents, generally mums, for whom additional support would make the difference between keeping or losing their child. I recommend watching the Post Adoption Centre video: *The forgotten voices of birth parents*. It acknowledges how having the right resources in place would negate the need for a number of modern-day adoption orders.

There is such resonance for me in hearing one of the mothers question the lack of support available to help her keep her child: '*They give adoptive parents this training that's so vital for them to be adopters, well why can't they give that to us? Because they're just training them to become parents aren't they?*'

It also appears societal judgement and shaming of mothers whose children are relinquished is still there, too. On the video I heard the same mother say: '*I've had my neighbours shouting through my windows – I've still got my kids – You ain't got your kids – you're worth nothing.*'

Back when I was 16, pregnant, unmarried, stigmatised and banished to St Anne's, a little compassion, kindness and love would have made such a difference to how I coped over the following 50 years. I'm sure this is true for mothers in the same position today too.

Chapter Fifty-Nine

Over the years, I have been fortunate enough to stumble upon a number of people who have provided me with excellent support, including the GP who encouraged me to retake my A levels, the psychotherapist at St George's in the late 80s, and of course, the renowned trauma specialist Dr Liz Hall whose work with me was transformational. I deliberately say 'stumble upon' as I was unaware of any specific specialist services on offer to mothers in my situation. It was luck of the draw, or my own research, that led me to them. Thankfully, my drive to do well at work also meant I could afford to pay for them.

What about all of the other mothers from the 50s, 60s and 70s who are struggling with their loss or navigating their way through the complexities of reunion, decades after relinquishing their children; mothers who don't know where to turn for support or don't have the financial means to access any services that may exist. How do people even find out what is available?

The Post Adoption Centre (PAC) sounds like just the sort of place where mothers like me could turn to for support. According to its website it offers 'specialist therapy, advice support, counselling and training for all affected by adoption and permanency'. It is rated outstanding by Ofsted. Yet when I rang and asked to speak to whoever is leading the services for first mothers, the person on the phone told me there is no-one with that specific remit, at least not at the current time. Perhaps they were just unaware of someone covering that area, but I was shocked and saddened to hear this. I would have expected to find a senior manager in post with the specific remit to design, develop and coordinate service delivery to 'first family' members across the UK.

On a more heartening note, there is a website page detailing a broad range of 'First Family Services '. This is where I found the video mentioned earlier. Having read through the listed services, I rang the advice line to enquire about the current 'birth mother' groups. I was delighted to hear about online groups and I was very keen to join one. I had always struggled to get to the annual meeting, now defunct, or the more regular drop-in meetings on the premises in North London, because of my travel issues. An online group would be an ideal way for me to access ongoing support. It also sounded like the meetings were regular ones. I was feeling upbeat.

The email reply to my enquiry said:

'Unfortunately, it seems you're unable to access our birth mother's group as you don't live in a subscribing local authority'.

So there you have it – I am not eligible for any support. My understanding is support via PAC is only available to people who have recently had a child placed for adoption and even then, is only available to residents from areas that fund this.

While I am delighted that there are support services for mothers who fit the criteria for access, I believe that every mother who has been affected by relinquishing their child or children to adoption should have access to centrally funded specialist support services.

I know of mothers who are still hoping to be reunited with their child; older than me and without that reassurance of knowing their child is ok. I know of others where the reunion has not worked out well for a whole variety of reasons. Not everyone who was adopted was brought up in a loving family or even knew they were adopted until much later in life. A lack of awareness of the circumstances surrounding their own adoption (or sometimes even with) may be a factor, or perhaps there's no support from members of their adoptive family, well-intentioned or otherwise. Emotions such as rejection, abandonment and anger understandably can run high. It could also be they are just not ready to meet their first mother, maybe out of loyalty to the parents who brought them up or for a myriad of other reasons. It must be hard at times for adoptive parents too, especially if they have their own insecurities about themselves, as most human beings do.

There are also first mothers who to this day have not told anyone about what happened to them; the need for secrecy still so much part of their fragile identity. These mothers may not know how to explain the secrecy or are unable to manage their emotions after having buried them for so long.

In all three perspectives – first mothers (and fathers), adoptive parents and adoptees – there will be people who are simply not coping with where they are right now. They are doing the best they can which can be so hard for the others in the triangle to understand, or handle themselves, especially when there is a mismatch with their own needs or expectations. Whatever the situation, it is always full of complexities and emotions that are unique to the people involved.

I cannot advise anyone what is best for them in their own situation, but I hope that following the enquiry, support services will be broadened to include opportunities for listening and learning from the other perspectives in the triangle. Personally, I have found it very beneficial not only talking with other first mothers but also listening to people who are adopted; I was interested to read a report from a round table session at the enquiry where a group of adoptees said they would have welcomed an opportunity to listen to the experiences of first mothers. I would also welcome the opportunity to listen and learn about the experiences and perspectives of mothers and fathers, who have adopted children from mothers who, like me, gave birth to their son or daughter in the 50s, 60s and 70s.

Justice is being sought in other areas related to adoption too. Alongside the adoption inquiry, campaigners in Scotland have been urging the Scottish Government to look into the use of Diethylstibestrol, also known as DES and Stilbestrol, Stilboestrol and Desplex, which as mentioned briefly earlier, was given to young mums in the UK to dry up their breast milk when their babies were removed. Though I have no clear recollection of it having happened to me, and I have not been able to see my medical records from the time, I suspect that I was given drugs to stop me from lactating after John was born.

Not only has this drug been linked to infertility, early menopause and cancer in the women who took it, similar conditions have been seen in their children and grandchildren too. Talking to the Sunday Post, Marion McMillan of Forced Adoption Scotland said, 'I remember being given 16 Stilbestrol tablets in one day, a huge amount. I'm now dying of cancer and it haunts me whether that drug had anything to do with my illness, or whether my children were affected.'

It's a potent reminder that adoption doesn't only adversely affect birth parents and adoptees. The effects of adoption cascade down the generations.

Hopefully, the parliamentary inquiry will bring a sense of closure to the many people involved. At the end of her speech to open the inquiry, Harriet Harman QC MP put it perfectly:

'The adoptions took place decades ago, but the pain and suffering remain today.'

What about my son? Has he been affected too? Has his adoption had lifelong effects on him that in any way parallel my own? The evidence presented to the Enquiry by adoptees is heart-breaking as they describe experiences of marginalisation and isolation and the profound long-lasting effects of maternal separation on their mental health.

Personally, I am not surprised by this at all. It makes perfect sense to me. John, my Baby Tim, came into the world and into my loving arms. For the first few weeks of his life he knew my touch, my smell, my voice. I was there to reassure him and soothe him when he cried. Suddenly, four weeks after he was born I was no longer there. Imagine how unsettling that must have been for him. When he cried he was held by strangers, first his foster carer and later his adoptive parents. Maybe he had just adjusted to the former when familiarity was taken from him again. At that stage in his life he was unable to speak out, unable to ask what was happening or to understand why.

It is now known that separation is a trauma and causes both mother and child to suffer spikes in adrenaline and cortisol as a response to the stress. Mothers cannot simply 'get on with their lives' and babies are not the 'blank slates' people thought they were back when Baby Tim was born.

My Baby Tim, my son John, was lucky enough to be adopted by parents who loved him dearly and guided him to be the fine man he is today. With his sisters and nieces he is, and always will be, part of their family just like a biological child. He is their son, their brother and their uncle. Despite this, I know our separation and John's adoption has affected him deeply, more than he first realised when out of curiosity he agreed to meet me in his adult life.

We see echoes of ourselves in each other, not only in the physical sense but in how alike we are in so many ways; ways that are hard to explain given the years we spent apart. Nature has an almost mystical power. We are connected and we have a sense of belonging together. We are pieces of the same jigsaw.

I know that me being back in John's life also gave him enormous challenges working out what to do for the best in terms of balancing seeing me and worrying about how our relationship might make his adoptive parents feel. This is such a terrible position for a child to be in. I can only speak for myself when I say there was zero threat from me to his relationship with his adoptive parents. I have nothing but the greatest respect for his mum and dad.

I take a very simple view. The more love a child has the better, and the more open things can be, the less stress there is for an adoptee to manage. I am very sad that John felt he had to compartmentalise things which made everything so much more complex for him. At the same time, having spoken to other adoptees who manage having two families in their lives in a similar way, I understand. Being an adoptee has its own complexities.

Chapter Sixty

For me the consequences of getting pregnant and my son being adopted have been like a prison sentence throughout my adult life: a life sentence, without early parole. My identity, my sense of self has been harmed. Do I even have a sense of self today? With so little memory it is hard to know who I am. All those milestone moments in life related to becoming a mother, I only know happened because there is external evidence to say they happened. I only know that I cared for my son, as his mum, for the first four weeks of his life because my files tell me so; I only know he was christened and that I was there because there are photos, fading and yellowing with age, that show this to be the case. And, perhaps because it was the trigger for everything that followed, I only know I had sex with John's father because I became pregnant.

I have spent the last 50 years living in turmoil. No matter what I have tried – eating, drinking, working myself to exhaustion, counselling – the pain has never gone away. It always felt like part of me, part of my soul, was missing. There was a huge void there and no matter what I did, I could not fill it. I was forever incomplete.

Being told that I should 'go away and forget and get on with my life' was never going to be possible. The bond between me as a mother and my child was too strong, just as nature intended. It is ludicrous that anyone, even back then, was unable to see this would be the case. I was too compliant and too naive to challenge this. I believed what I was told.

As I said earlier, I believed I had a choice. Fifty years on I realise this was an illusion. Interestingly, I mentioned this to Dr Mike Lambert and this is what he said:

"Your reply about having the 'illusion of choice' is very revealing. I think this is right. In order to push back against the different welfare authorities at such a young age you would have had to know an awful lot about your own legal rights, entitlements and potential sources of help. These were not easy to find. Intentionally so. Part of this was about trying to have a deterrent effect: to prevent other unmarried mothers by setting an example of those that 'chose' to do so. Even with the maximum amount of financial support – which was at its peak during the late 1970s before it was reformed under the Conservatives – it would still have been incredibly difficult. It was for so many, hence the scale of poverty experienced."

The cards had been dealt. The outcome was set at the outset. John's first-father Tim put it so well when I spoke to him only recently, 'We were on a conveyor belt. Every time we asked to explore the possibility of keeping our son, or perhaps having him fostered until we'd left school and had found a place of our own, we were gently nudged back in the direction of adoption. We were constantly reminded that we had to do what was "best for the baby" – never referred to as "your baby" – and made to see our natural instinct to want to hold on to our child as being somehow selfish.'

Whenever I asked for time or information, the answer was always 'yes, we need to look at that', but there was never any follow-through. No-one ever came back to me. I believe no-one ever had the intention of coming back to me. I was never given any information on supplementary benefits, available at that time. No-one talked me through my options or outlined how I could be supported to keep my child. Indeed, on the very day I asked for more time, 12 days after giving birth. I was given forms to sign that included the questions asking about my consent to adoption.

My 'value' to the many people involved in the adoption of my son ended the day I was sent the form to be taken and signed in front of a magistrate. There was no follow up. No-one checking in with me to see whether I was ok, how I was coping or whether I needed any help dealing with my disenfranchised grief and the challenges of keeping everything secret from everyone. Even both sets of parents just sighed with relief. It was over, their reputations had been protected. I was expected to go back to my life as it was before and carry on regardless. As far as the adoption agency was concerned, I was discarded, no longer of any value – I had served my purpose providing a child to a deserving and respectable married couple.

Can you yourself imagine for a minute, giving birth and having *your* child taken away from you either immediately, or in the first few weeks of his or her life? I'm sure for most, the very thought of the possibility of this happening is a nightmare. How would you manage having to pretend that you've never been pregnant in the first place? Or being rejected and abandoned by the very people from whom you expected love and care? Being banished, having to remain out of sight for fear of the shame that you have caused? Would you be able to part from *your child* and keep everything under wraps, not being allowed to show or express your pain and grief from the loss or even tell anyone you had had a child without fear of repercussions? And what about as your child got older – how would you cope with not knowing where they were, what life was like for them or even if they were alive? How would you cope and survive?

I am no longer a practising Catholic. The association between my child being taken from me and the Church is too strong. I only have to see a nun and I'm running in the opposite direction. I respect people who have faith and gain richness in their life from this by walking the talk; people like Emma and her husband who showed me such kindness and compassion while we were in hospital having our children together. I have no time for hypocrites – people who go to church on Sundays but, once outside, treat people badly. I can't bear people who get caught up in status or think themselves 'better' than others. Or worse still people, who in the name of God, appear to be able to justify their bigotry.

The people dealing with us 'bad girls' at any stage of our pregnancy, through giving birth or the adoption process must have gone back home to their own children. I will never understand how they could begin to think that their behaviour in terms of what they dished out to us and how they treated us was acceptable. Never in a million years would they have dreamed of treating themselves or their own children like that. It is shocking, it is disgraceful.

In many ways I consider myself to be one of the lucky ones. I was a mum to my son for the first four weeks of his life. Although I don't have a single memory of ever having held him, fed him, bathed him or changed him once back at St Anne's, for me it is still better that I know that I did care for him. A number of women never got to see their baby at all before they were taken away, or were told they could see their baby later only to find them already gone.

I hope what I believe to be true, really is true, as I hang on to that knowledge like gold dust. I can never be totally certain though as swapping babies between mothers and giving each another child to care for was a practice I've been told of. I'm cautiously confident given my file says how attached I was to my baby. I also look at one of the photos from Baby Tim's christening. I can see all the love and joy in my face as I hold my son in my arms and look down at his beautiful face. Every time I look at the photo I am tearful, but what I see there also sustains me, especially when the sadness of the last 50 years overwhelms me. I look at that photo and I see myself. I am Baby Tim's mum. I had everything I needed for this to be so.

One thing that really annoys me is when people seem to think: *'you're back together now, everything is healed'* or *'it's a happy ending, how wonderful'*. Of course it's wonderful that we are reunited but nothing and no-one will ever be able to give us back what has been taken from us. There are so many precious moments in a child's life that are a marvel for parents to share. John and I were denied the opportunity to share these moments together.

My son and I were parted for 28 years. That's 28 years of me not knowing where my son was, how he was, or even if he was alive. The experience was terrible and at times sheer agony. It has impacted every aspect of my life. That is not something that gets healed simply by being reunited.

Yes, please be happy we are together but just make sure you stay away from indicating to me that everything should be great now, that we are both suddenly 'fixed'. We are not. I find myself feeling so angry when 'well-meaning' people, even family and friends, stray into that territory. We've both had a lifetime of experiences apart; we parted as mother and baby, we reunited as mother and adult son. Since we were first reunited there have been many complexities and sensitivities for us to navigate. We have both done a fantastic job but it has not been easy or straightforward. It has taken a lot of work. We have had to take things slowly. There have been many times where it has been one step forward and three steps back.

A huge struggle for me was the ongoing secrecy and at times, having to remain hidden from existence as John's mother. I would start to relax and let myself enjoy the emotion of motherhood, only to find that I had to go back into my all too familiar cupboard and be hidden away from the world.

My memory loss is also massive for me, probably more than anything else. The majority of my recollections are compiled from old records, photos or from talking with John's first father, Tim. Very little of my experiences surrounding my pregnancy and the adoption is in my head as conscious memory; often there are just fragments. From my work with Dr Hall, I know the memories are there physiologically but no matter what I've tried, including hypnotherapy, not even a glimmer appears. Why can't I have just one memory of holding or feeding my son back at St Anne's? This also makes me wonder about what I don't know about. Did other things happen to me during my pregnancy, the process of adoption and afterwards that are not recorded anywhere and I don't even know they happened?

The physical and mental scars are still with me; the challenges of living a life with so many secrets and lies forced upon me. Living with the shame of what I had done. Being abandoned and rejected by those from whom I expected unconditional love. So many years of coping with anxiety and the agoraphobia triggered every time I am faced with travelling to anywhere unfamiliar, or sometimes even to the familiar, especially when I'm alone. Times when even being alone in my own home at night has been like a nightmare. So many years of trying to bury the pain for all the loss in my life. And so much more… There has been a cost. I now have very limited capacity to deal with any stress in my life. Everyday stressors that used to be water off a duck's back can affect me for days, especially physically. The good thing now is that I recognise this. Whereas before I would have pushed myself through, I now take time to recover.

From 1990 until just a few years ago, I have had a number of periods, each several weeks long, when one side of my body just didn't want to work – with pins and needles and a staggering gait. At one point there was a concern that I had MS, but I'm pleased to say MRI scams have ruled this out. I've not tracked the episodes but I suspect that there is a link to my past. I'm surprised my body has coped as well as it has in its adrenaline and cortisol fuelled environment. Long may that continue.

I have work to do. I still need to grieve for all those pivotal moments in my life: for the agony of being separated from my child, for all the precious moments between mother and child stolen from me, for my second baby that never was, for my parents, the tragic loss of my sister taken at such a young age, and most importantly, for the loss of myself or at least the part of myself that was lost for 50 years.

But it's always taken so much energy to be me and now I feel I have little in reserve to draw on. Maybe that's the key here. Perhaps I need to draw on the practice of mindfulness instead and 'just be'.

Chapter Sixty-One

The strangest duality about my life is that despite all the pain and sadness and my lack of self-worth as a mother, or even as a human being, I am energised, engaged, passionate and confident about whatever I get involved in. I always give of my best and I gain real enjoyment from everything I do. I also do everything to the nth degree; my friend Julia pointed out to me how much I love learning and my need to become autonomous in whatever I turn my hand to via professional qualifications. Those characteristic qualities so evident in me as a young child, have not only survived but flourished.

My journey in life has been such an interesting mix. I have gone from living in a house that should have been condemned, to partying the night away at Annabel's and flying on corporate jets! In my work life I have been a cleaner, a cook, a lifeguard. I have milked cows, worked as a holiday tour guide and as a shop assistant. Later on I had careers that took me to the upper echelons, the upper floors reserved for senior management, in roles that were always seen as 'outside the box'. Along the way I also studied nutrition, taught Tai Chi and qualified as a Pilates teacher just after my 60th birthday. Currently I teach a particular genre of photography and I'm on a five-year course which will have me qualifying as a Medical Herbalist when I am 70. What a hoot really. I am a funny old soul. I have done all of these things despite being paralysed at times with anxiety and phobias – literally – so that I'm glued to a spot, dizzy and feeling like it is hard to breathe, or being consumed with sadness and pain. I have pushed myself hard.

Pushing through my complete fear of flying on commercial flights, I have been to China, Russia, Lapland, the East Coast of the States, the Caribbean and most of Europe. I have sailed across the Channel and in the crystal-clear waters of the British Virgin Islands. Despite my phobias and anxieties I ran my own business successfully for 15 years, without clients ever being aware of my difficulties. It makes me laugh when I think back to someone saying to me 'you are the most together person I know'.

Both my parents experienced total upheaval early on in their lives and came to this country with very little. No silver spoon for members of our family. Whatever any of us achieved it was down to us plus a good measure of fate, such as my father being able to leave the Siberian labour camp and surviving the sinking of the Empress of Canada. My parents' experiences instilled in me my sheer determination and drive, my love of learning and my instinct to survive, no matter what.

After my sister Anna's death, my mother's forgiveness, silent in words but strong in her actions was the catalyst for shifting me into realising the value of everything my parents had given me, despite the difficult times between us. My parents valued every day they had. My father abhorred war. Their happiest times were in their little cottage, surrounded by the beauty of nature. Nature gave them solace as it does me. My parents taught me the importance of being grateful for life, to be appreciative of what you have and never to be acquisitive.

Subsequently I have also learnt another lesson – things are not always as they appear because reasons that explain why people behave as they do are often hidden from view. Going through family papers after my father's death, I discovered yet another secret. I found out that my Mum was at least six months pregnant when she and Dad were finally allowed to get married. No wonder she was as harsh on me as she was. Whenever I'd asked my parents for the date of their wedding anniversary, I would be fobbed off. I'm certain Mum would have experienced a lot of hostility towards her given she was both an unmarried pregnant woman and an immigrant. The former in and of itself, could have led to her deportation given the annual reviews she had to pass in order to stay in the UK! Marrying my father gave her a lot more than avoiding an 'illegitimate pregnancy'.

If I had known this earlier it would have gone a way towards me understanding why my mum was so adamant that I was not keeping my son in my unmarried state! That would have helped me a lot, as it has done now that I do know. My heart goes out to my Mum. I'm sure she carried in herself so many other things which she would never speak about. She, like me, buried things away. Unlike her, I am moving towards some kind of inner peace by bringing everything out into the open, giving me the freedom to live authentically.

I am at peace with my parents now. Given the pressures on them I accept their actions were in keeping with what was expected of them at that time. The harsh moral climate with the fear of judgement and being ostracised within their own community would have been especially hard for them given their own backgrounds and life experiences. People in authority telling them adoption was the best way forward for all concerned would also have been a significant influence on their attitude and behaviour. They did the best they could. From what I have learned of their circumstances, I genuinely think they had my best interests at heart too. I think Mum more than anyone could see what a difficult road lay ahead for me and felt her stance would protect me. My only wish is that at least one of them would have held me tight and told me that everything was going to be all right, that they would be by my side.

The aphorism of Nietzche, 'What doesn't kill you makes you stronger', has a ring of truth to it. In my case I was judged harshly and shunned by society and by my family at a crucial age; 15, an age where self-identity development is taking place. I have never felt that I fit in, anywhere. That doesn't mean I don't get involved in my local community, far from it. I led the development of our local Parish Plan for three years, I set up and chaired our local patient participation group, I helped to secure funding for a wildlife pond and so on. The key thing is I look for things where I can make a difference but can work in my own way. I'm fine when I am creating, designing, developing and leading projects as I'm using my expertise. I'm in a space where I have always been proud of myself. As long as I can stay away from having to be in social situations where I need to relate to people that I don't know well, I am fine.

Having said this, I love helping and supporting people, to be the best they can be, whether I know them well or not. I have discovered that coaching and facilitating learning for others are my special niches in life. I love being a catalyst and enabler. I hate injustice or people being held back by their circumstances. I love seeing people succeed, especially people who have worked hard to overcome disadvantage or adversity to do so. I suspect part of this is being able to empathise with people starting out or facing challenges in their lives and give them skills, support and encouragement. I know these things would have made such a difference to me.

Friends are particularly important to me and I am blessed. With my closest friends we have formed deep and strong bonds; we are there for each other through thick and thin – these are my friends for life and people I trust completely. Most I have known for many years and they have helped me enormously, as has my sister. I like to think that I am a good friend and a supportive sister too, being an advocate, helping and championing what each person needs, as well as just having fun together.

Overall, despite everything, I like my life and I like where it has led me. I am resourceful and I have such a zest for living. I have survived. I have more than survived.

Writing this book has been quite an undertaking both in terms of time but also emotionally. I have been on a journey of discovery as there was so much to piece together. First and foremost I wrote this book for myself. I needed to find a way of taking the time and space to face things head on. For 50 years I had tried so many strategies, some of which had worked well, others less so but never in such depth as my explorations here.

I know exactly what it is like to live as a secret and not be free to be who I am, openly, or indeed, even to know who I am. Please when you read this, spare a thought for anyone who is struggling with their own sense of identity or grappling with loss. As long as no harm is being caused to another, help people to express themselves, to be themselves. Embrace diversity. When you meet someone new, or even people you think you know well, just remember, they may be facing all sorts of struggles in their lives that are hidden from view. Kindness, compassion and understanding go a long way.

I also feel mine is an important story to be told, not just for me but for all the mothers from the 50s, 60s and 70s. Mothers who have faced having their child adopted simply because they were unmarried; mothers, who for this reason alone, were shunned by society and seen as 'bad girls', and unfit to keep their child.

Most of the stories to date have concentrated on the circumstances surrounding the pregnancy and what happened leading up to the adoption. I wanted to take this story much further. I want people to understand how mothers like me are still living with such deep pain. The consequences are so far reaching and not only for us. In many ways the day our children were taken from us is only the start; the start of a lifelong struggle to find ways to survive, and aim to still thrive, the best way we can.

There have been several times along my own journey where I felt I was heading towards rock bottom. A number of the choices I made to handle things with myself in order to survive did me more harm than good. Self-sabotage and a tendency to catastrophise are still things I need to watch out for. Like everyone, I was doing the best I could at the time, without the gift of hindsight and I am doing the best I can today. I am proud of myself.

This book would never have come into being without the support of my son. I am grateful for his encouragement and his steadfastness in wanting my story to be told. I have been braver as a result of this in terms of what I have shared with you as readers. I have gone from being a secret to being an open book and that is scary!

Epilogue

Fifty years on, I am filled with gratitude that my son and I have been reunited and we have navigated our way successfully through the rollercoaster ride of reunion. John and I are pieces of the same jigsaw and our reunion has brought those pieces back together. It's complex, it's inexplicable at times, it's emotionally challenging but as far as I am aware we are both so much more at peace and complete now that we are back in each other's lives.

I am so proud of my son, John. Over the years we have been together again I have seen just how fine a person he is. First and foremost he is kind, compassionate, honest and fully of integrity. The loving care towards both his parents was so wonderful to see. He always shows such care and consideration towards me too. His wider family loves him deeply and he them. I see the great husband and father he is; coparenting to raise his daughter, treating Liz with respect and recognising the equal importance of her career alongside his own. They make such a great team.

Within all of this he has excelled himself professionally and academically too. He has all the values and qualities I would wish for in a child. Now, I can see exactly what his mum meant when she said he had fulfilled his potential. And my father's words about being grateful to the parents who brought him up and what a good job they did, ring true. It has been a long journey for me, and for John and I to be back together, but if I had to do it all again to be where I am, and where John and I are today, I would do so gladly. My parents and their forebears would be so proud of John too.

The keys to our successful reunion have been respect, patience, the strength to handle the bumps along the road, giving and taking time for personal space, being able to judge when the time is right for more deep and meaningful conversations, positive intentions, having fun together and taking genuine delight in just getting to know each other, as we are today. I am lucky that John is as lovely a person as he is and that we both entered into our journey together with positive intentions and a desire for it to succeed. As I covered earlier, I am one of the lucky ones as not everyone is reunited and not all reunions are successful. This must be terrible.

Although it is very sad that both of John's adoptive parents are no longer alive and naturally the grief still endures, we are now free to come together. I can be acknowledged publicly for who I am. I am no longer a secret!

Where we are now came home to me so beautifully just a few months ago. I was invited to lunch and found myself around the table with John, Liz, my granddaughter, Jo and her husband, and Jane – Jane joining us via Skype from New Zealand. The room was full of laughter and chatter and warmth and thanks to Liz, delicious food. I had the sudden realisation this was the first time we had been together without any need for secrecy. I felt this inner whoosh of emotion that told me just how profound this day was for me; another time for tears, but this time happy tears gently bubbling up to the surface.

After our meal Jo invited me to walk round to the nearby house where her father, John's father, had lived in the last couple of years. She wanted me to 'meet' him, and for him to be part of this special day with all of us together. Standing in his house suddenly we had our arms wrapped around each other and were both moved to tears, as I am again as I write these concluding paragraphs.

We shared how we felt and how happy we both are that I am now free to be in John's life openly. Such a special day for so many reasons. I felt at home. I was there as part of their family which is now part of my family too.

I still have a lot of healing to do. Old habits, particularly my lack of confidence with my granddaughter and the residual effects of so much trauma in my life are still there. These things will take time to settle but I have such hope for what the future holds. After 50 years I'm finally able to be myself, to find myself. I may be one of two but I am John's mother. I am also a grandmother now. I am no longer a secret. I can step out from my cupboard for good and begin to build a sense of identity in both these roles. For my son and I, this is our time. Our window of time in life for us to be together and to do so openly. For me this is awesome.

Acknowledgements

I would like to say thank you to my husband. With you as my partner in life, I am flourishing. It is wonderful to be loved by you just the way I am and to be connected strongly by what's important in life and by our values. You always seem to know just when to wrap your arms around me and hug me too. I am blessed to have you in my life.

I am fortunate to have such special friends in my life with a number of friendships that have endured over several decades. I love every one of you deeply. You know who you are even if you've not been mentioned in the book explicitly. Maria, Linda, and Julia, as well as being such dear long-standing friends, who have been with me every step of the way since we first met, I'd like to say a special thank you to the three of you for your specific support and help to me during the last few months while I've been writing my book. My book is so much better because of your involvement. Pat, I'd also like to thank you and your family for all your support over the years, drawing me into your family and giving me a sense that I would have been a great mum. Chris, your singing and song writing coupled with your sense of fun and good humour have helped me so much along the way too!

Thank you to my sister for your support with writing my book. It is lovely we are good friends now and value having each other in our lives. I enjoy our time together. Mum and Dad would be so pleased and proud of us. I love you and your family.

To everyone in my son's family thank you for your support and for everything you have each done, and continue to do, to help us reunite. I'm loving getting to know you independently too. My life is much richer for us being part of each other's families.

And to John's first father, Tim. Thank you for your support to me over the years and for your help with my book. It is lovely we have stayed in touch. I know you are sad about what happened. You need to be proud of yourself for everything you did at the time. Thank you for being by my side as much as you could.

I would also thank Dr Michael Lambert, of Lancaster University, for the time he spent helping me to understand the social policies, attitudes and practices surrounding me in the early 70s. Our conversations have had a positive impact on me, far beyond simply including some of what he said in the book. It is good to know that the enquiry 'The Right To Family Life: Adoption of Children Of Unmarried Women 1949 – 1976' is drawing on your expertise in childhood studies, public health, sociology and now social policy. It will be all the more robust for this.

Thank you to Eve Hatton, Jo Sollis, Mel Sambells and the team at Mardle Books for helping to bring my story to publication. As a first-time author I was nervous; the integrity and genuine care for me by the team, especially by Jo, made all the difference. Thank you also to Chris Manby for being such a great mentor and guide. Without you, this book would not be here today.

Acknowledgements

Finally to my son, thank you for being so willing to build our new family relationship after our long separation. You are loved by so many as a child, brother, husband and father and I am proud to be part of this family circle. I love you, I'm proud of you, and you mean the world to me.

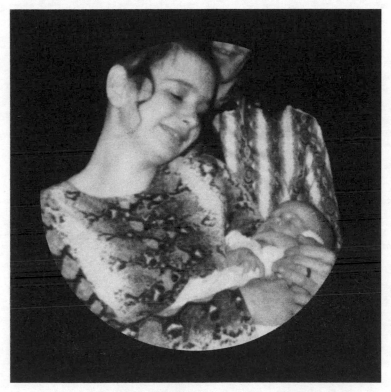

Michelle with her baby son, Tim